Welcome Aboard

By

Victoria Farnsworth

Copyright © 2014 by Victoria Farnsworth
All rights reserved.
ISBN-10: 1494893533
ISBN-13: 9781494893538

Dedicated to My Family
without whose love this story could never have been written.

Contents

Preface

EVERY PERSON BORN who has the opportunity to sojourn on the earth has a story to tell. We are all unique individuals. Some lives are short lived; others endure for decades. The length of time we spend here does not make our story worth telling; it is what we do in the amount of time we are allotted that begs to be documented for posterity or the rising generation to learn from and grow.

Beginning with my first book, Welcome Aboard, I relate stories from my life that have left indelible impressions on my soul. My body, mind, everything about my personality has been shaped and molded by my life's experiences. Many of these stories are humorous and light-hearted; some are tragic and full of sorrow. They all beg to be told! Be mindful of the fact that these are memories of mine as a very young child. I cannot remember every detail; only those that made a distinct impression on me. The sequence of the chapters and even some of the events within the chapters may not be in the order that they actually happened. These events were so many years ago, I cannot possibly remember every aspect. They are, however, written as I recall them.

My father was an officer in the Navy. I barely knew my father when I was a child, yet I have always loved the ocean and everything nautical. Fresh water lakes and rivers are appealing, but my passion has always been the sea. With that in mind, you are about to embark on an amazing voyage.

Welcome Aboard!

CHAPTER 1

In the Beginning

BEFORE I BEGIN my story, I must first introduce you to my parents who are both deceased. I think it is important for you to understand a little about my mother and father so you can better appreciate how I came to be who and what I am. (When I reflect on the idiosyncrasies of my parents, I am amazed that neither one of them ended up in a mental institution before they were 30!)

My father, Warren Van Pelt (born in 1910), was the eldest of three boys. His mother left his father and the three young boys when my father was only 10 years old. (It had very negative and life-long effect on him and his relationships with women.) Grandpa was a farmer in Illinois, and Warren and his brothers grew up doing farm chores; they were accustomed to hard work. Grandpa remarried soon after his first wife left him, and Pearl became mother to the boys and eventually became the grandma I loved.

The farm wasn't earning a profit, so the family packed up and moved out west to California. My father ended up spending his last two years of high school in Garden Grove, California. As soon as he graduated, he joined the Navy and was off to see the world (and get away from farm life)!

My mother, Eleanora Irene Lesco (1924) was born of immigrant parents who had met and married in Chicago. Her father, William, (born in Romania) was a candy maker, although he must have done a lot of baking as well. (If it was a sweet confection, he made it!) Her mother, Mary, (born in Hungary) worked in her parents' grocery store. My mother went to work full-time when she was only 12 years old. She worked for her parents, and on occasion, worked for her aunt and uncle in their store in New York. Eleanora spent most of her teenage years back and forth between the two cities, working in the retail business. She did attend school and managed to graduate by the time she was 16.

My mother's parents divorced when she was in her early teens. When she was 16, Eleanora, her sister, and her mother, along with lots of aunts and uncles, moved caravan style from Chicago out west to California. My mother went to work for the Navy as a welder, and in her off hours, worked as an extra in Hollywood. (She was a stand-in for Lucille Ball.)

My mother seemed to fall in and out of love quite often. She was married and divorced twice before she met my father. They married in 1945. Mom had a son from her first marriage (my oldest brother Jerry) and then she and my father had a boy (my full brother Warren) a year after they were married.

You may think this story of my parents sounds pretty normal and they shouldn't have any real idiosyncrasies. That was not the case! Now I will give you a glimpse of just what I was born into.

My father didn't trust women and really didn't even like them. He was attracted to a pretty face and they had to be a lot younger than him. (The older they got, the less he was attracted to them.) He was also very into his own likes and interests and couldn't care less about anything my mother was interested in. He was very self-absorbed and, of course, wanted to further his Naval and singing careers. (I have not yet mentioned that my father had a very good baritone voice and actually sang semi-professionally. He sang on the radio and for special occasions in the Navy.) To be honest, he was a very talented individual, just not good husband (or father) material.

Eleanora was a very artistic, creative type of person. She could sew, paint, build, and do all sorts of crafty things. She would see something she wanted, and if she couldn't afford it, she would figure out a way to make it. In that respect, she was absolutely amazing!

However, my mother had phobias! She was terrified of water deeper than her waist. She had been taught from an early age that you wade out to waist deep water and then swim toward the shore or shallow end of the pool. She wasn't very tall, 5'4", so she never learned to swim more than a few strokes at a time. She was also deathly afraid of heights! It made her nervous to step up onto anything higher than her knees! Last, but certainly not the least, was her fear of birds. Heaven knows what had caused that strange phobia, but it bothered her throughout her life.

At this point, you may be wondering what these idiosyncrasies have to do with me. That thought is a perfect place to begin my story.

My father and mother were required to attend a social gathering on board the ship my father was assigned to. I was due at any time, but my father was adamant that my mother attend. Unfortunately, the only way to get aboard the ship was via a gang-plank type contraption with ropes on either side to hold onto (my mother's description). The side of the ship was high above the dock and the make-shift boarding platform was at a very steep angle. My father, of course, walked right up with no problem. Mom, on the other hand, was facing her worse fears. Seagulls were flying overhead and underneath! Mom's eyes registered the distance above the water at about 60 feet. The wobbly plank was about 25 feet long. (These are my mother's estimates. Who knows; she always liked to exaggerate.) The water beneath was very deep; how would she survive such an ordeal?

She managed to get aboard with no mishaps. No sooner had she sat down in a chair offered the poor pregnant lady, when her contractions started! Everyone, including my father, thought that was very funny. Well, not everyone. My mother wasn't laughing at all!

Mom had to muster every ounce of courage she possessed and with the determination that only a mother can achieve, she gingerly made her way back down that horrible plank! My father, as usual, had to stay a bit longer and talk with his superiors, joke with his crew members, and make sure everyone knew that he had been in attendance. He then disembarked and found my mother sitting in the car, trying to be brave and not show her complete frustration.

Off to the Mare Island Naval Hospital we went. I was about to make my appearance! After a very long labor, my mother gave birth. I would like to say I was a bouncing, baby girl; but in reality, I was very tiny and a bit on the fragile side. I was born August 11, 1949 at 1:00 pm and weighed a scant 4 pounds, 15 ounces. I was full-term but destined to be petite. (Usually children grow taller than their parents; not me. At my tallest height, I measured 5 feet and one quarter inch. I always tell people that my mother smoked and it stunted my growth.)

Since I cannot remember anything about my life during these very early years, I've got to rely on what I've been told. My mother was the only person that ever shared anything with me about this time in my life, and she was an extreme exaggerator! Truth or fiction, I cannot tell; all I can do is relate the stories she shared with me.

My mother was a smoker! Nowadays we know how bad it is for children to be exposed to second-hand smoke, but when I was little, no one really took notice. Her bad habit rubbed off on my oldest brother and he was trying to smoke by the time he was seven! Mom thought it was cute and no harm because he didn't inhale. (My brother died of lung cancer when he was only 63.) My fragile little body couldn't deal with the environment around me. I had my first battle with pneumonia when I was only 4 months old! (I don't think the doctors at that time associated it with my mother's incessant smoking, but to this day I am extremely allergic to second-hand smoke and suffer severe asthma when exposed.)

My parents had just moved from California to Bainbridge Island, Washington when I was four months old. Even to this day I wonder if part of the pneumonia problem was because of the change of climate and vegetation. I was allergic to so many trees, grasses, weeds, and food. What a life for a little girl! (Of course, we didn't know I had these allergies until several years later; instead, I just suffered.) My father got a job at the Winslow Hardware Store and sang on the radio in Seattle. He was in the Naval Reserve and didn't go back into active duty until the Korean Conflict. My mother was busy with young boys and a baby girl. She was a stay-at-home mom.

My brothers did take a lot of mom's time. Jerry, the oldest, was always running away. Mom said he had the wander lust. When he was only 5 years old, while they still lived in California, he went missing and they found him on board one of the ships! On Bainbridge his wandering continued. The neighbors were all warned to keep an eye open for the little dark-haired boy who insisted on seeing the world. My brother Warren had emotional problems.

I'm not sure if he was born with problems or if they were a result of circumstances beyond his control. My parents divorced when I was only two years old. My brother Warren was five; it surely had a profound effect on him. I don't think it bothered my oldest brother because he was always wandering off and happy to be away from home. I was too young to care and I can't remember anything about that time. But Warren, my only 100% sibling, had mental problems.

Warren had a pet pig. I don't know the pig's name but my brother loved him dearly. One day mom informed him that they needed to take the pig to Winslow. My brother got all excited because his friend got to go to town. They brought the pig in a small trailer attached to the back of the car. My brother rode up front with my mother. They went to a shop and talked with the man in the white coat. Then they left the pig with him. Mom told my brother they would come back and get him in a few days. Horror of horrors, when they went back to get him, he was all cut up and wrapped in little packages of white paper! My brother cried all the way home and didn't want to eat pork for many years!

CHAPTER 2

The Terrible Twos

I HAVE NO personal memory of this year. I know my parents were divorced and my mother remarried shortly thereafter. I know that I suffered with two bouts of pneumonia and that it would plague me all through my early years. My mother didn't even have any Terrible Two stories to tell of this time in my life. So, let's get on with what I do remember!

CHAPTER 3

Three Years Old and Three Brothers

As PREVIOUSLY MENTIONED, Mom remarried shortly after divorcing my father and we got a step-dad. I don't believe it bothered my brother Jerry because my father was his step-dad too. I'm sure it bothered my brother Warren because he adored his Poppy. For me, I got a dad. He adored me and I got a whole new family of aunts and uncles, cousins, and grand-parents! Life was good!

Of course, I remember nothing of this early time in my life. My memories don't begin until the day before my little brother was born. It was two days before my third birthday. I know very few people can remember their really early years, however, that day and night have remained with me throughout my life (now 64 years later). From this point on, there will be no more retelling stories from my mother. The following are all first-hand experiences, written as I remember them.

Dad swooped me up in his arms and carried me out to the big Pontiac. Mom followed, bag in hand. I didn't know where my brothers had gone; I'm sure they were at a friend's house for the night. I was going to my Aunt Virginia and Uncle Stanley's. (Life was so good!) I was so young and surely hadn't been there very often, but everything was so familiar and I knew it was a safe, happy place. My cousins were there (they were much older than me) and my Uncle was the closest thing to Santa Clause I knew. What a treat for me to be spoiled by these wonderful people I loved!

However, the unexpected happened! Mom gave me a big hug and kiss, and then, she and my Dad left me there! I absolutely had a panic attack. I remember crying, actually throwing a tantrum and sobbing so uncontrollably that I couldn't even hear what my Aunt was saying to me. I could not be consoled; my mother had left me. True, I loved the people I was with, but I had never been away from my Mom before and suddenly these people seemed more like strangers than family. My heart was breaking; I was scared and didn't understand what was happening.

Aunt Virginia finally calmed me down by offering to make chocolate chip cookies. Even at my young age, I had a definite chocolate addiction. The way to my heart, was over my taste buds and into my stomach! Mmmm! I can still smell them baking and remember the sheer joy of eating warm cookies with a glass of milk. I sat on the little red high chair and thoroughly enjoyed myself.

I remember having dinner with the family and not being hungry. I was full of cookies and milk and I was missing Mom very much. I was definitely apprehensive about the coming night and what was going to happen to me. This was so much for a little person to deal with!

Upstairs at Aunt Virginia and Uncle Stanley's were the bedrooms of my cousins. On the west side was the boy's room and on the east was the girls. I was shown the upstairs (up a very steep, narrow stairway) and where the bathroom was at the bottom of the stairs. (I guess no one wanted me to have an accident in the middle of the night.) So far, so good; I was calm and adjusting to my predicament quite well. Unfortunately, my composure did not last.

When it was time to go to bed, I was assigned to sleep with my cousin Joan. Her younger sister Sylvia was in the bed across the room. I started crying. Both my cousins kept trying to calm me down and were really kind and understanding (for a while). However, after half an hour or so, patience wore thin and I was told in no uncertain terms to stop crying and go to sleep!

They asked too much of me. How could I, so frightened and alone, go to sleep away from my mother? What would happen during the long night? What would happen the next morning? I was just so afraid. I worried my little self to sleep and longed for life to be back to normal.

Day finally dawned and I was awake and up early (even for me). I had survived the night and now I was ready to go home! (Even now I can't remember anything about home; just that I wanted to go there.) After breakfast,t I helped gather eggs from the chicken coop and had fun petting the goat (until he began eating my shoe). There were carrots to pull from the garden and beans to pick. It was sure fun at my Aunt and Uncle's house!

After the morning chores were done, the phone rang. I got to talk to my mother. I had a baby brother! I remember being disappointed because I thought it would be much better to have a little siste,r but I was happy because I would get to go home pretty soon and tomorrow was my birthday! Who cared about a little brother; I was going to be three years old tomorrow!

That's all my memory serves me. I can't remember my birthday at all! I don't know if I celebrated it with my older cousins or if I got to go home and spend it with my family. I'm sure my two older brothers would have loved to have cake and ice-cream but I can't remember one detail of that day. The stress of staying the night with my Aunt and Uncle and then the fun of the animals and garden was imprinted so deeply in my memory that all else from that time faded away. I vaguely remember staying another night, sleeping in the big bed with my cousin.

CHAPTER 4

The Big House

I CAN'T REMEMBER the little house I first lived in on Bainbridge Island. I believe the area was called West Port Madison. I do remember our neighbors who lived down at the beach, good friends of my brothers and my parents. There was also a single lady who lived next door to them who became my special friend. But my memory of these wonderful people are from after we moved into the Big House.

I can't remember the actual moving day. But I do remember just after moving in, my friends came to see me. My friend Cheryl, her brother Bobbie, and her cousin Stevie came to my big new house. Stevie was a little boy who was my same age and was plagued with allergies and asthma too. I remember our mom's sitting in the big living room talking about our breathing problems and his mom saying they were thinking about moving to Arizona. That meant nothing to me; I had a big new house (it was an old hospital) and I got to show my friends all the rooms!

There were lots of rooms. On the main floor, there was a kitchen, a funny little room mom referred to as the office, a long hall way that extended the length of the house, two bedrooms, a bath room, a huge walk-in closet, the living room and dining room. On the north end of the house, there was a laundry room that was actually an enclosed porch. On the south end there was a porch that was really the formal entry way. The whole west side was a long, narrow, covered porch. There was a wonderful stairwell that housed two flights of stairs. (It was a great place to play as the years went by.) Upstairs there was a huge room that became the play room. There were five bedrooms and a storage closet that eventually became a bath room. There were also two large storage closets off the bedrooms at either end of the house. They were actually attic spaces. (Two more wonderful places to play as the years went by.)

As a young child, the house seemed huge and it was my pleasure to take my guests on a magical tour of this amazing place. They were awed by the size and so many places to hide. It was truly like a childhood fantasy only it was real!

My room was downstairs at the south end of the house. Originally it had been the surgery when the house was a hospital. There was a sink in the room, and Mom thought that seemed like a very clean, sanitary place for her fragile little daughter to stay. My doctor had told her to keep me away from dust, so the fact that a sink adorned my room, made her think that need was met.

I, on the other hand, wanted the room upstairs on the south end of the house. I could see the water of Puget Sound and the Olympic Mountains from that room. My girlfriend Joanie lived in the little house across the field and I could wave to her from out the window. I insisted and Mom gave in. She thought I would be afraid up there so far from her but I informed her that I was a big girl (my little brother Davey was one) and that it was time for me to be on my own! My older brothers were upstairs too so I wasn't really alone. My dad painted my room pink and put in a new, blue linoleum floor. I loved that room!

The big house wasn't the only wonderful thing on that property. We had six apple trees, a ton of plum trees, a grape vine, and the most amazing peach tree. The peach tree was really old, but it had huge, giant peaches that were juicy and sweet. Ymmm! I didn't have any allergy to fruit and I indulged! Mom and Dad planted a vegetable garden in the back yard. It really produced. (It was planted over the septic drain field!) At the time, I didn't know about such things; I just knew that we had plenty to eat and life was good.

I don't remember how long we had lived in the Big House when I first saw a ghost. I didn't even know it was a ghost. I didn't know about such things. I just remember waking up one night and looking toward the end of my bed to see a man standing there as if he were looking out the window. I didn't want him to see that I was awake, so I pretended to be asleep and kept my eyes just closed enough to still see him. I started to be afraid and covered my head. When I peeked out a little later, he was gone. It couldn't have been my dad because he was away in Alaska fishing. I told my brothers the next morning and they told my Mom. We were all on the lookout from that time forward.

That Big House became a wonderful home. I was so happy there even though I had serious problems. My allergies were bad and I continued to have pneumonia twice a year until I was eight. There were happy times and sad times in that house; times that are recorded in my memory as though they just happened yesterday.

CHAPTER 5

Bottle of Joy

MY BROTHER DAVEY had a lot of serious problems. Sure, I was plagued with allergies and asthma, and I had my seasonal bouts of pneumonia, but my baby brother had much worse problems. Something was wrong with his head! I was too young to know what the matter was but I knew it was bad. His head was shaped really weird! It was almost flat on one side and his eyes were looking in opposite directions!

He did all the things you would expect a baby brother to do. He cried a lot, dirtied his diapers, and made a complete mess when Mom fed him. (I just knew if I had a baby sister she wouldn't do any of those horrid things!) He crawled in an odd sort of way, but I was told babies scoot around any way they like.

I, on the other hand, was such a good little girl. (Just ask me!) I was four years old and I had outgrown my potty chair. It was time to start using the big toilet. I was extremely small for my age so I needed a little stool to step on so I could sit on the toilet and then get off again without having to slide down to the floor.

One day I decided to try and get on the toilet without the aid of the little stool. My dad saw what I was doing and asked if I could do it. Of course, no problem; I was a big girl now. So he left me and went out of the bathroom, leaving the door to the hallway wide open. I struggled to boost myself up onto the toilet seat by standing on my tiptoes, back facing the seat, and using my upper arm strength. I did it, although I thought for sure I would fall flat on my face!

That task accomplished, I proceeded to take care of business. I was just finishing when I heard my mother scream. I looked toward the hallway and saw my dad running toward the kitchen end of the house. Next my mother went running by in the opposite direction, carrying my baby brother. My dad went running by like he was chasing her and then she ran back toward the kitchen again. My dad was following close behind. My brother was crying really loud and I was sure there was something coming out of his mouth.

I was anxious to know what all the commotion was about, but I had to get off the toilet to find out. The floor was a long way down! I hung on to both sides of the seat, slid my bottom slowly toward the front of the seat, and let my toes stretch to find solid ground. There wasn't any! I had no choice but to drop if I wanted to investigate the commotion in our kitchen. Kerplunk! I landed on all fours, but I did it! No more stool for me!

Mom was hysterical; screaming all kinds of 4-letter words and at the same time praising God. At least, that's what it sounded like to me. I later learned that Mom wasn't praising God; she was using the phrase to express her feelings. The expression, "Oh My God," was her most often used phrase in the English language! My dad was trying to console her while at the same time cradling my baby brother in his arms. My baby brother was crying and foam was coming out of his mouth!

Mom calmed down enough to phone the doctor. From her side of the conversation, I learned that my bothersome baby brother had drank a bottle of Joy Dishwashing Liquid. I looked around and sure enough, there lay the empty bottle on the kitchen floor in front of the sink cupboard where he had found it. The whole kitchen smelled like lemons; it must have tasted as good as it smelled.

The baby-sitter was called and she came over after Mom and Dad already left. I got to tell her all about the excitement. She said everything was going to be fine and we cut out paper dolls.

Mom and Dad came home about an hour later and baby Davey was fine. Mom said the doctor pumped out Davey's stomach and that he would be OK. After that, I didn't mind so much when he cried or made a mess. He just was too young to know any better.

CHAPTER 6

Christmas at Grandma's

ON CHRISTMAS EVE we went to the big family Christmas dinner at Grandma Henderson's house. We lived in Seabold, on the north end of Bainbridge Island. Most of the relatives lived either in Seabold or in nearby neighborhoods. A few lived as far away as Seattle! It was such a magical, happy time of year.

Grandma's house smelled yummy when we walked into the warm kitchen from the back porch. (Even as a small child I wondered why we always entered the house via the back porch into the kitchen and never entered through the front door into the living room.)

Grandma had a big wood-burning cook stove that stood on four legs. It was huge! There were warming ovens up above the cooking surface and there was a huge oven beneath. On the side, was the firebox. You could feed wood into the fire through a door on the front of the firebox or through one of the two lids on top. You could cook anywhere on the surface of that huge stove! When you needed a hot spot, you moved the pot over the firebox; if you needed low heat just to warm something, you moved the pot to the other side of the stove. I loved to sit in Grandma's rocking chair by the wood stove and feel the warmth penetrate my body. From that lovely chair I could see all the delicious deserts waiting their turn to fill the buffet table.

Grandma had a new bathroom on the back porch! We didn't need to use the outhouse in the back yard! That's a good thing because it was cold and dark outside! It was cold in the bathroom too! We would rush back into the kitchen and wash our hands in the big sink that had a pump for the water! Grandma's house was the only house I knew that had a pump for the water. (I vaguely remember my aunt's house having a pump, but I can't be sure. Sometimes in my mind's eye I see pumps in other kitchens, but it was so long ago and I was so young, it is hard to remember.)

When everyone arrived and greeted everyone else, dinner was served buffet style in the dining room. My cousins and I got to choose what we wanted on our plate and an adult would put it there for us. (We really didn't get to choose at all. I distinctly remember Aunty Ariel saying to me, "Would you like some turkey? White or dark? Why don't you have a little of both. Would you like some mashed potatoes and gravy? Here, just eat that much. Do you want some green beans? Sure you do.") When I wanted lots of olives I was told I could have three for now and more when I finished my dinner. When our plates were full, we were escorted to the kitchen to eat at the "kids' table."

My cousins and I had fun at the kids' table. We could be noisy, messy, and bad-mannered and no one cared! Of course, we were dressed up for Christmas dinner so we tried to not be very messy. We could hear the grown-ups in the other room laughing, talking, and thoroughly enjoying themselves. (I think they were drinking something they didn't want us to know about. I saw a bottle of something that looked and smelled like grape juice. I heard Mom say something about Mogan David and even at that young age I figured it was that bottle of grape juice.) We got milk to drink. We would dare each other to take a bite of cranberries and then a drink of milk. Oh my goodness! It was so terrible, it felt like your teeth would curl! We also enjoyed putting olives on our fingers and eating them in order. (That's why you needed more than three!)

After we finished eating, it was time to open presents. There was so much excitement and anticipation! We had presents waiting for us under our tree at home and Santa would be bringing presents too. But here, under the big tree at Grandma's, there were presents for everyone! Oh what a delightful time to be a little girl in this wonderful big family! I got presents from so many aunts and uncles; how could they have known just what I wanted? My cousins got gifts they loved too. Everyone was happy; each saying thank you and if they could see what the other person got. There was so much love in that warm, cozy house with all those wonderful people.

After the gifts were opened and the wrapping and ribbons cleaned up, came the moment everyone was waiting for. Dessert! There were cakes, pies, tarts, and cookies. I knew just what I wanted. Mince-meat tarts. I just knew that pretty little pie with only a crust on the bottom would taste so good and melt in my mouth. But alas, my Aunt Ariel said they would make me sick to my stomach. How could that be? I could smell them and they smelled exactly how I wanted them to taste! I had to be happy with apple pie until my aunt wasn't looking and I sneaked a tart. I gobbled it down so fast because I didn't want to get caught. What I could taste I loved and have craved them every Christmas since.

Oh my goodness! What did I hear? Was it jingle bells? I'm sure I could hear jingle bells. It had gotten really quiet, and as I looked around the living room, I could see looks of amazement on the faces of my aunts and uncles. I looked at my mom and dad and they were looking amazed too. Could it be? I was afraid of Santa Clause at the big store in Seattle, but was he coming here? Shouldn't he be out delivering presents to all the good little boys and girls around the world who were fast asleep in their beds? I held my breath in anticipation. Sure enough, the front door opened with a blast of cold air and a jolly, "Ho, Ho, Ho!" It was Santa Clause! He had stopped by just to say hi and find out exactly what we wanted for Christmas. (He also needed some sustenance in the form of cookies and milk.) (Odd, even to this day, I was sure he was my uncle Stanley!)

After an evening like the one I had just experienced, how could I be expected to go to sleep? I wasn't the least bit tired. We drove the short distance home and went into the big house. Our Christmas tree was still there, the stockings were still empty, and mom and dad seemed unusually tired and wanted to go to bed. My older brothers and I just looked at each other and thought, "Might as well 'cause morning will come sooner if we go to sleep." (At least baby Davey was asleep.)

My brother Warren was the first one up on Christmas morning and yelled for everyone to wake up 'cause Santa had been there. I scrambled down the two flights of stairs, the back of my PJs letting in a cool breeze. I wished I could stay warm. I went straight to the big floor register and stood on it, eyeing the treasures hidden in the stockings hanging from the fireplace mantle. There were more presents under the tree! Santa had been there!

We could get into our stockings right away, but we had to wait to open our gifts from Mom and Dad, and of course Santa, until Mom and Dad had Davey up and ready to enjoy the day. (I'm sure if I had a baby sister the wait wouldn't have been nearly so long!) Finally we got to open our presents. I got PJs without a bottom flap, slippers, and a bathrobe! Wow, I was going to be warm now! But the best present in the whole, wide world was waiting to be unwrapped! (I could tell by Mom's face that I was going to love it.) I unwrapped the biggest doll I had ever seen! She was as big as me. She had long, blonde hair and blue eyes just like mine. She was wearing a dress that had a red and white striped blouse and a dark, blue skirt. She had on white ankle socks and black patent leather shoes. I knew her name instantly because when asked I said, "Suzabella."

Chapter 7

Suzabella

THIS MARVELOUS DOLL was all mine! I knew my big brothers wanted nothing to do with her, and my baby brother was too young to even know she existed. My goodness, how lucky could one little girl be, to have a doll as a playmate! What fun playing with her. She would do everything I wanted. I could make all the play rules, decide what she would wear, when she would take her nap, and when she would go to bed at night. I was the mommy and the friend all in one!

It was rather difficult for me to carry Suzabella from one location to another. After all, I was extremely small for my age and she was a very big doll. She didn't weigh very much; it wasn't that she was heavy. She was just cumbersome. She had long legs and arms that dangled when I carried her. I was always tripping over an arm or a leg when I carried her. I did try to carry her like a baby (my dad showed me how) and it worked pretty well until an arm would slip out of my grasp. There had to be a better way.

My dad showed me something I used time and again, feet on feet walking. I just put Suzabella in front of me facing forward with her feet on mine. I held her close to me and leaned my head to the side so I could see where we were going, and away we went. This method of transportation worked really well as long as we stayed upstairs or downstairs to play. When we needed to go up or down the stairs it was useless. (Not only did I use this method playing with Suzabella, but also with my younger siblings as they came into our family. I again used it with my own children when they were small.)

I loved to slide down the railing. It was hard for me to attempt to get onto the railing with Suzabella, so I decided she could slide while I walked. I would stand at the top of the stairwell, in front of the railing that kept us from falling off the second floor down to the first floor. The top flight of stairs was to the left, and the bottom flight was to the front and beneath where I stood. I pulled Suzabella up and got her situated on the railing with her legs and arms hanging over each side. I kept my left hand on her back and moved over to top of the stairs, and then put my right hand on the railing. I had to reach across in front of me to keep my left hand on her, but the responsibility to see to her safety was my main concern. It did not matter to me that the situation was awkward; I was a very good mommy! We gingerly made our way down the top flight of stairs. When we got to the landing, I helped her off the railing and we sat on the floor at the top of the lower flight. She sat beside me, like my very best friend, and we proceeded to make our way down to the main floor. I would scoot my bottom to the edge of a stair, and with the strength of my legs and my right arm, lower myself down to the next step. Then I would help Suzabella down to the stair beside me. We used this mode of travel for at least a couple of years!

Going up stairs was the opposite of coming down. We began at the first bottom step; both sitting side by side. I would push myself up using my right arm and both legs. Then I would help Suzabella up beside me. When we reached the landing, I would lift her onto the railing, put her arms and legs on either side, while holding onto her with my left arm. My right arm reached across and held the railing and I slowly climbed while pushing her up. Sometimes we used the sitting method on the second flight; it just depended on what decision I made at the moment. I never gave Suzabella a choice!

Suzabella spent a lot of time with me that winter and spring. I had pneumonia and she was right beside me in bed getting well. She got well without getting a shot of penicillin or having to drink lots of fluids, or smell stinky socks! What a lucky friend she was.

Chapter 8

Stinky Socks

I HAD THE extreme misfortune of having to endure an old-time remedy for sore throats and, in my case, pneumonia. I guess my mom thought that if the treatment was good for a sore throat, it must be good for your lungs. (She had a lot of strange ideas.) I can tell you from first-hand experience, it does no good for either!

I remember laying on the sofa in the dining room. Mom wanted me there so she could be working in the kitchen and keep an eye on me at the same time. I had Suzabella laying down with me. I did have a very sore throat that had absolutely nothing to do with the pneumonia. Mom was anxious for Dad to come in the house (he was working under the house in the basement) so she could try her remedy. I couldn't figure out why he needed to be in the house. He was working on a project for my big brothers and I'm sure they didn't want him to be disturbed. (To get to the basement we had to go outside and follow a little walkway around the Laurel tree do the side door. The basement wasn't a basement as we know them today. It was really a crawl space that an adult could stand up in the front half.)

Dad finally came into the house and Mom asked him for his dirty socks. I remember the conversation between them as if it were yesterday. He didn't think it would work; Mom was sure it would. He was a devoted husband and father, so he went along with her plan and supported her when I fought tooth and nail!

Mom bent over me with a foul smelling, off-white sock in her hand. It wreaked like my oldest brother's tennis shoes! She wrapped the sock around my neck and pinned it on with one of Davey's diaper pins. Oh, it was awful! I kept trying to get away and crying because the smell was making me sick to my stomach. Dad kept telling me to stop crying and breathe deep because it would make me feel better. Mom was practically sitting on me to keep me there on the sofa. (Today that would have been labeled as child abuse.) In my mind, at that time, it was abuse and I would not soon forgive them!

My breathing got worse! The fact that I was crying probably didn't help matters, but the smell was making it impossible for me to breathe. (To this day, when I smell certain things, I still get asthma.) My parents thought they were helping me and they were making me sicker than I already was! Pretty soon Mom gave up and took the horrid thing from off my neck. Then she called the doctor.

The next thing I knew I was being carried to the Pontiac (Dads big car). We were off to the Winslow Ferry for a trip to Seattle so I could go to the Children's Orthopedic Hospital. (I had been there several times in my young life, but this was the first occasion I remember clearly.) I didn't want to go to the hospital. I cried all the way on the ferry boat, and all the way to the hospital, through the busy streets and steep hills of Seattle. Mom was afraid of the traffic and steep hills and that was scaring me too. I kept wishing we could just turn around and go home. I was having a hard time breathing and that was really scaring me!

CHAPTER 9

Iron Lung

WE ARRIVED AT Children's Orthopedic Hospital with no mishaps. That was surprising, even to me, because of the steep hills and heavy traffic. I had never seen so many different kinds of cars, trucks, and buses as on that trip to the hospital. My dad carried me into the hospital, with my mom following close behind. Her apprehensiveness was frightening more than my difficulty breathing. Even at my young age, I knew she was a worry-wart and an exaggerator, so I wondered if I was really as sick as she was behaving.

We went to the big front desk in the reception room. I had been there before because it seemed familiar, yet I couldn't remember when I had been there. I loved looking at the paintings on the walls and ceiling. Even the big floor was very colorful. It was quite welcoming for a child. A nurse brought a crib on wheels into the reception area and my dad put me in it. Oh, the humiliation! I was much too grown up to be in a crib! Things progressed rapidly downhill from there!

I was wheeled into a large room with another crib in it on the left side of the room. Straight ahead were a lot of large windows, but my crib was put near the doorway, instead of near the windows. I wasn't happy about that. I would have loved to look out the window and see the big city. On the right side of the room there were two large, round, long tube-like contraptions. I had no idea what they were, but there was a child inside each one! Their heads were out and they greeted me when the nurse carried me over and introduced me. I can't remember the girl; she seemed not interested in me at all. But I do remember the boy. He was a lot older than me and had a beautiful smile with perfect white teeth.

He had dark, curly hair and was so happy to meet me. I asked him what that thing was he was laying in. He told me it was an iron lung.

I was struck with fear. Until then I was coping; trying to be brave, and putting up with all the grown-ups making me do what they wanted. But I recognized the words, iron lung! My mom had told me again and again to not walk or play in the mud puddles. She said I would get Polio and that I would have to breathe in an iron lung. She said I would have to spend my life in a wheel chair, or walk with leg braces and crutches. Here I was, having a hard time breathing, and I was face to face with two kids in iron lungs! Up to this point in my life, my asthma seemed to be caused from things that smelled bad to me, or that I was allergic to. But right then and there, I felt like I couldn't breathe!

The nurse who was carrying me realized I was having more difficulty breathing. She put me in my crib and left immediately. She came back momentarily with a cart holding lots of strange things. There was another nurse with her and a very young nurse wearing a striped uniform. They worked quickly, making me my own little tent to play in. The nurse in the striped dress had some toys in a box and she let me choose a couple to play with inside my tent. The nurse gave me a control with a button and said to push the red button when I needed something. The nurse told me I would be comfortable and could breathe a lot easier inside my little tent.

The nurses left me to play quietly with my little toys. I had a little, curly-haired doll and a wooden toy truck. The nurse in the striped dress came back into the room with some little dresses for the doll. She said she thought I would like those better than the truck and she was right. (I hadn't entered my tom-boy stage yet.)

I kept looking across the room at those iron lungs. I was glad my tent was see-through so I could keep an eye on things. Unfortunately, the iron lungs were directly across from me, and that's what I had to look at. I couldn't see anything out of the windows except the sky, and it was cloudy. I hoped I wasn't going to end up in one of those iron lungs. I kept hearing all sorts of noises coming from them. It made me nervous, but I pretended everything was fine and played with the little doll. I must have changed her clothes a dozen times. She only had three dresses, but I tried them all on her again and again. When a nurse looked in, I pretended everything was fine, smiled, and continued to play.

What seemed like a very long time passed, and my mother walked into the room. She first looked towards the iron lungs and then at me in my little tent. She gasped, put her hands over her mouth, turned, and ran out of the room. I could hear her crying, "Oh My God!" Of course, that undid all my bravery, and I started to cry. Crying made it more difficult to breathe and the nurse came in to calm me down. I could hear another nurse out in the hall with my mother, telling her to not act upset because she was frightening me. I heard her say that I was in an oxygen tent, and it was helping me to breathe.

Mom came in a few moments later and acted like it was so fun to visit me in my little tent. She had on a gown over her dress and gloves that went a long way up her arms. She could reach her hands in through these two openings in my tent and play with my doll or brush my hair. When my mom was calm, she was such a joy to have close by. I loved her a lot!

I couldn't eat. To be honest, that didn't bother me because I wasn't one bit hungry. To my horror, a nurse came in and said she was going to give me something to eat. I didn't see a plate of food on her little cart; only a bottle of what looked like water and some tubes, and a huge injection needle. I knew I didn't want what she had to offer! She pulled up the dress I was wearing. (They made me wear a dress that came from the hospital. I got to choose one from a rack when I first got there and every day I got to choose a clean one to wear.) She then informed me this would feel like a bee sting, and proceeded to insert that huge needle into my leg. I was as brave as I could be and tried not to cry. She attached a tube to the end of the needle, and used a bunch of tape to hold it in place. The tube was attached to that bottle of water she hung on a hook. It reminded me of the coat rack at home. It was on wheels, so when she had to carry me somewhere, she could pull or push it along beside her.

I honestly can't remember how many days I spent in the hospital. I think it was only about three. The nurses took good care of me and carried me around a lot. I thought they just carried me because they liked me. Years later I figured out that walking would have caused me to need more oxygen and they were taking really great care of me. Mom visited me once during that stay; it was hard for her to come to Seattle when she had three boys at home. Friends and family were always willing to help out by watching the boys, but my brothers were a handful. Each of them had problems of some sort, and my poor mother was always at her wit's end! I was too young to realize what my mother had to deal with on a daily basis, but thinking back, it's no wonder she had a breakdown years later.

CHAPTER 10

M & M's

MY DAD AND mom drove a big, black Pontiac. I loved that car. Behind the back seat, in front of the rear window, was an area just large enough for me to lie down. (We didn't wear seat belts in those days.) I could lie there and watch the clouds zooming by as we sped down the highway. I could see the tree tops or birds flying overhead; a few times I even saw planes! My two older brothers were too big to ride up in the window seat, as I called it. My little brother was always on Mom's lap, or if she were driving, he was in the car seat up front. (In those days there were no rules about babies not being allowed to sit in the front.)

To keep us quiet on long drives, Mom always brought food for us to eat. I would lie on my window seat and enjoy peanut butter and jelly sandwiches or cream cheese and jelly (my favorite). I never worried about choking; I didn't even know what that word meant.

On this particular day, I was up in my window seat. My older brothers were not in the car. My little brother was on Mom's lap and Dad was driving. I can't remember where we were going. I didn't have a sandwich to eat, and I started complaining that I was hungry. Mom said she had a treat for me. She reached down into her bag and came up holding a brown candy baggy. It was M & M's. She ripped open the corner by holding the edge between her teeth and pulling on the baggy. (I always tried to do that but never succeeded until a few years later.) She popped a few of the M & M's in her mouth and passed the baggy back to me. I had to climb down off the window seat to grab the baggy. I climbed back up to my lofty domain, and stared up at the sky, as I partook of the sweet delights one by one.

In those days M & M's only came in the color brown. They were coated in a brown chocolate shell, and inside the chocolate melted in my mouth. I could let the shell melt, or chew it so I would get to the soft chocolate faster. I loved chocolate; there was definitely no other candy that compared! I was enjoying the sweet, luscious taste as it melted in my mouth. Instead of waiting until one completely disappeared, I popped another in. Pretty soon I was popping M & M's much faster than I was devouring them; my mouth was getting quite full! All of a sudden, I couldn't breathe!

I panicked and rolled off the window seat onto the rear seat. Mom looked back at me and screamed, "Oh My God, she's choking!"

Dad very quickly stopped the car and jumped out of the driver's seat. He opened the back door and grabbed me so fast, I didn't know what was happening. First he slapped me on the back to get me to cough, but I couldn't cough because I couldn't take a breath of air. The next thing I knew, he bent my waist over his arm, grabbed my feet, and hung me upside down. He again slapped me on the back, and the big chocolate wad of melting M & M's landed on the road beneath my head. I got a big breath of air and cried, "My M & M's!"

Dad turned me right side up and set me down. He scolded me for putting so much in my mouth at a time. I felt humiliated and ashamed. I had done a naughty thing and had scared my mom and dad. (They didn't know how scared I was and how sad I was that my M & M's were lying in a little brown pile on the road.) I climbed back up into my window seat and rode the rest of the way in silence, broken hearted because I had no more M & M's.

CHAPTER 11

Easter 1954

MY MOTHER WAS an excellent seamstress. She made almost all of my clothes, especially my dresses. Easter was a time when little boys and girls got new clothes to wear to church. This year, Mom was going to let me select the fabric for my Easter dress; I was so excited!

We went to the fabric store and looked at all the pretty bolts of fabric on display. Mom kept trying to interest me in little flowers or butterflies; they were pretty but they just weren't right. Oh my goodness! I found just what I wanted; it was checked! This beautiful bolt of fabric had peach and cream checks. They were one inch squares of soft, silky fabric; fabric like nothing else I had ever had. (I can still remember Mom and the lady who was helping us laughing because they thought that was such a funny choice.) But to me, it was beautiful. I loved peaches and cream, and that dress reminded me of one of my favorite desserts.

I remember Mom altering a pattern for my new dress. (She always had to cut things way down or make a pattern on her own.) She bought a pattern for this dress, and it became a pattern for lots of dresses for the next few years! When she began cutting the fabric, she said lots of four letter words. The fabric, it seemed, was inclined to run, snag, and do all sorts of other bothersome things while she attempted to cut it. She had trouble sewing it too; but she was a wonderful mother, and was determined to make my dress.

Mom chose a piece of cream-colored fabric to make a large, square c on my new dress. The dress was so pretty. It had short, puffed sleeves, collar, and a full, round skirt. It was perfect and I loved it. My talente also made my petticoat for underneath and lots of nylon netting g waste of elastic to keep my skirt spread out around me. She bought me white ankle socks with ruffles on the tops, and black patent leather shoes. To top off the whole ensemble, she bought me an Easter bonnet with a matching purse, so I could wear the ribbons and flowers she wanted. My Easter outfit was still not complete until Mom added the white gloves. I had never been so decked out in my entire life! I felt like one of the pretty dolls in the department store window.

Easter Sunday came and I was excited to go to church in my pretty, new outfit. I was sure mine would be the prettiest Easter dress anyone had ever seen. Mom seldom came to church; I always went with my Aunt Jessie and cousins' Neal and Carol. But this was a special day, and Mom came with me and took my baby brother. When we got to church, I was surprised by all the pretty dresses! Everyone looked as beautiful as me. What a happy day. Everyone was in their new dresses, looking so pretty with their hair in curls, and wearing Easter bonnets. (I didn't pay any attention to little boys at that time.) I cannot remember anything about the church service that day; I can only remember how pretty everyone looked.

The next memory I have of that day was after church, when we went to visit Mom's friends who lived near our old house in West Port Madison. We drove down a long, narrow driveway to a house near the beach. The house was surrounded by a grassy field. It was mowed near the house to look like a lawn. There was a cow munching grass between the house and the beach. She was tethered to a pole, and seemed very content. (Everything seemed familiar to me, as though I had been to this house often. Yet, this is the first memory I have of it.)

I wanted to go down by the water; I loved the water. The lady who lived in the house told me to be careful where I walked because there were cow pies hid-

ss. I told her not to worry; I would watch where I stepped.

careful because I was wearing my beautiful Easter outfit
nen to it. I began the walk to the beach. It
skirted around the area where the cow was
to close to her. In my eagerness to get to the
ful where I stepped, I didn't pay attention to
orning dew was still quite heavy and the grass

was wet and slippery. There was a slight downgrade toward the water, and the wet grass caused my patent leather shoes to slip out from under me!

I landed on my bottom, still wearing my beautiful new Easter dress, right in the middle of a cow pie! Horror of horrors! That nasty, stinky stuff was all over my shoes and socks, my legs and petticoats, my dress, and even a little on my gloves. My bonnet was spared the humiliation, and I didn't have my purse with me. I cried; I felt so horrible! I wasn't hurt in the least, but I was mortified by the experience! My mother and her friend were up at the house, watching the whole episode unfold before their eyes, laughing as hard as I have ever seen my mother laugh.

I walked back up the little hill to my mom and she took me into the house where she and her friend had me take off my soiled dress and petticoats. They cleaned me up enough to get into the Pontiac and go home (laughing all the while). My pretty dress came out of the wash as good as new and I wore it many more times. I did learn a few lessons that day. One, always be careful on wet grass; two, looks are only skin deep, and three, laugh at what life throws your way!

CHAPTER 12

Sunday School

EVERY SUNDAY MORNING my Aunt Jessie and cousins would come by to take me to Sunday school. Seabold had a wonderful little community church and all the relatives that lived on the north end of Bainbridge Island attended that little church. It was non-denominational and we did not have a minister. Men from the community took turns giving us a sermon. (Even to this day, having been a member of both the Methodist for several years and the Mormon for almost 50 years, I have no sweeter memories than those early years when I attended the Seabold Community Church.)

The spirit was strong! I was so young, I didn't know what that really meant; all I knew was that I was happy there. The feelings of love and belonging crowded out any feelings of shyness or loneliness. My family didn't attend with me; I always went with my aunt until I was old enough to walk by myself or with friends. I wanted my family to go with me; everyone else had their family with them. Thinking back, I realize now how blessed I was to have relatives that cared and loved me enough to ensure that I had a spiritual upbringing.

At this early age I had little interest in what was preached from the pulpit. I did love stories about Jesus and I believed the preacher when he said that Jesus loves everyone. I also believed him when he said that Jesus died so that I could live forever. I had no idea what that meant, but it sounded like Jesus loved all of us very much to do something so brave and wonderful. I loved Jesus!

What I enjoyed the most about Sunday, was when the adults were excused to go to their Sunday school class, and the children were left in the chapel to have singing time. One of my aunts, or another of the nice ladies, would give a short lesson about Jesus or the commandments, and then we would sing. One of the ladies would play the piano and another would teach us songs about Jesus. We sang about doing good deeds and keeping the commandments. We learned about the Bible, and about stories from the Bible, just through singing songs. What a wonderful way to learn!

There were always motions to go with the songs. We would use our hands and arms, stand up, sit down, jump up, and turn around. That singing lady kept us so active and busy, we didn't have time to misbehave! We just sang and laughed and learned lessons that have lingered a lifetime!

We learned that Jesus taught using parables. A parable was a story that could be understood by little children one way and by adults another way. He told the very same story, and whoever listened to it, would understand it the way he or she was able to. Jesus was the best teacher that ever lived!

One of my favorite songs was called, "The Wise Man and the Foolish Man." That song was about a parable Jesus told. When I learned the song, I learned a lesson about how sand is a poor foundation to build on and that rock was solid and a sure foundation. A few years passed before I understood that the sure foundation was the gospel of Jesus Christ. It didn't matter to me when I was so young. What mattered was the joy I felt in being there with the other children, singing songs I loved, and creating memories that have remained with me my whole life. The foundation of my spiritual life was being laid, line upon line and precept upon precept.

CHAPTER 13

The Post Office

NEXT TO THE Seabold Community Church was our little Post Office. It was painted gray and white, just like our church. The two buildings looked like they belonged to each other. In a way, they had similar benefits for the community they served. They both provided a place to meet and greet friends, we received good messages from both, and there was of course, a feeling of love that permeated from them.

You might think that feeling of love rather odd emanating from a post office, but I will tell you why I felt that love every time I went there. My grandma was the Post Mistress! Sometimes when we went there, she had cookies waiting for us. I knew she gave them to all the children that went to the post office. To me, however, it felt really special, because she was my grandma. She would finish her work of sorting the mail early in the day and then walk home to her house.

My favorite time to go to the post office was when she was ready to leave for the day. Mom would drive the Pontiac to the post office and pick up our mail and drop me off to go to Grandma's house. Grandma and I would walk the quarter mile, or so, until we reached the Community Hall and then take a left turn to walk through the woods to Grandma's house. I always thought of Little Red Riding Hood when we would walked through the woods to her house. I was never afraid of a big, bad wolf coming out from behind a bush; it was just the fact that we were walking through the woods to Grandma's house.

One day at the Post Office, I met a little girl named Judy; she was older than me. She called my grandma, Grandma! I was shocked; I didn't know this person and she was claiming my grandma as hers! My mother explained to me that my dad's sister, Virginia, was married to Judy's Uncle Stanley, which made my uncle her uncle too. Families are so complicated and this was way too much for a 4 year old to comprehend. It didn't really matter; here was someone else I could play with. But she lived too far away to walk to her house, so we really didn't play together often, until we were older. However, once again, the Post Office was the place to meet and greet people and to receive good news! I had a cousin and she had two brothers, so I had three more cousins I didn't even know I had!

Another time at the Post Office, I met a girl whose grandpa owned the chicken farm behind the Post Office. She was just my age! She had an older brother and her mom was a good friend of my mom's. Our mom's arranged for us to play together. They would get together and drink coffee while we played with our dolls. Not many months later, we were walking to each other's house. By this time, I knew for sure that the Post Office was a really important place. You made so many new friends there!

CHAPTER 14

Chicken Dinner

ONE DAY AT the Post Office, Mom met up with my friend's grandpa. She asked him if he had any chickens slaughtered and if she could buy one for dinner. He said, "Sure! Just come by in a few minutes."

We finished our business at the Post Office, and climbed into the Pontiac. Since we were just going to the driveway next door and then a short distance, I rode in the front seat. My little brother was in the car seat between my mom and me.

When we arrived at the farm house, my friend's grandpa came out of the house and walked over to the chicken yard. There must have been a hundred white chickens running around in that fenced-in yard. He asked my mom which one looked good. She gave him a funny look and asked what he meant. He informed her that he was going to chop off the head of the one she picked, and then we could take it home for dinner!

She picked out a chicken, and he went into the yard and caught it. He carried it into a shed, we heard a quick cluck and a whack, and that was that! He came out with a dead, headless chicken. He had some old newspapers to wrap it in and then he put it into the trunk of the Pontiac. My mother and I were both shaking as we drove silently home. My little brother Davey didn't even know what had just happened.

I did not want to be in the kitchen to observe that horrible task. Usually I was full of curiosity and would do whatever needed to be done to know what was going on. (Need I remind you of the bottle of Joy?) However, on this occasion, I wanted to be as far away as possible. I went outside to play on my little swing beneath the Crab Apple tree. After some time, I wandered back into the house to see how much progress had been made. I was getting hungry for fried chicken; my mom was a really good cook!

To my complete dismay, my mother was sitting in the middle of the kitchen floor. She had newspapers spread on the floor all around her. She had a large pot of very hot water in front of her and she was dunking that chicken in the water and then pulling out its feathers! She was exclaiming in 4-letter words her extreme dislike of the task before her. Even to my young eyes, it looked like we would have a very late dinner that day!

We usually ate dinner around 6:00 pm; Mom did not call us to dinner until 8:00 pm. (That was the latest I ever remember eating dinner as a child.) The fried chicken was just as good as it always was! We had mashed potatoes with gravy, carrot and raisin salad, corn bread, and apple crisp for dessert. Mom was the best cook ever. She made that chicken taste like it came straight from the grocery store! My older brothers were very upset that they hadn't been with us when we got the chicken. They were so envious of me because I got to be there. It was certainly an interesting conversation around the table that night.

CHAPTER 15

Good-Bye Joanie

MY BEST FRIEND in the whole world lived right next door to me. There was an old, wooden gate at the corner of the field next to our side yard. Joanie's house was in the center of that large field. Mom would walk with me to the gate, and Joanie and her mom would walk along a trail through the field and meet me at the gate. Then I would walk with them to Joanie's house. Mom would go back to our house; I can't remember her coming to Joanie's. I'm sure Joanie's mother was helping my mom by watching me so that mom had more time to spend with my little brother. (He was such a problem!)

I only remember that Joanie was my best friend. I really can't remember playing with her at her house. The only reason I know I played there often was because of the day I'll never forget. Mom walked with me all the way to Joanie's house! There was a truck at her house and two men were just finishing putting things into the truck. Joanie's dad was there; that was really strange because he was always at work. Joanie was crying and her mom was telling her everything was going to be OK. I got really worried when I saw Joanie crying; I knew nothing was OK!

Mom started hugging Joanie's mom and Joanie's dad was acting like they had to hurry. He put some suitcases into the trunk of their car and said, "Let's get a move on!"

Joanie's mom said to her, "Say good-bye to Vicki; it's time to go." Joanie turned to me and threw her arms around me. It suddenly dawned on me that Joanie was leaving for good.

"Don't go," I cried. But it was to no avail. The grown-ups didn't care that two little hearts were breaking. We both cried and clung to each other, vowing that we would never forget one another, and promising that we would be friends forever.

I watched Joanie get into the back seat of their old car and her mom get into the front seat. Her dad walked around to the driver's side, climbed in and shut the door. They all rolled down their windows and waved as they called, "Good Bye, God Bless!" Joanie drove away and part of my broken heart felt like it went with her.

I was sobbing uncontrollably, and mom said we had to get home. My dad was fishing in Alaska, so mom was really busy taking care of the house and four children. We no sooner started to leave, when a car drove down the driveway, and parked in front of us. There was a man, a woman, and five boys! The man got out and introduced himself to my mom. The woman rolled down her window and introduced herself and wondered why I was so unhappy. Mom explained that I was so sad because my best friend had just moved away. I can still remember what that lady said. "Oh, don't worry, you will have plenty of other kids to play with!"

I looked in the back seat of that car. It was stuffed with boys! I just wanted to get out of there and go home as fast as I could. I was missing Joanie. I needed Joanie, not a bunch of stupid boys. If I wanted boys, I had three brothers already. My two oldest brothers didn't want to be bothered by me and my little brother was too little; I didn't want to be bothered by him! I certainly didn't need a bunch more boys in my life; what was I going to do?

CHAPTER 16

The Tribe Moves In

MY WORLD TURNED upside down in an instant! Five boys had moved in next door. My best friend in the world was gone, and I was surrounded by boys. Who was I going to play dolls with? Suzabella was still near and dear to me, but I was a very sociable child and needed, in fact craved, the interaction with other children. I had some other girlfriends, but they lived too far away for me to walk to their houses. Mom didn't have time to take me or go and get them to come to play with me. If I wanted playmates, it was going to have to be with one or two of those boys next door!

I remember the first day I decided to go and see what they were like, and see if I thought any of them could fill the void I now had in my life. I let myself through the gate, and walked to Joanie's house all by myself. I went right to the front door that was open and looked inside. They were all in there, making all sorts of racket. Five boys can really make a lot of noise! They were all having trouble finding their shoes, clothes, and asking where this, that, or the other was. Their poor mom was beside herself, and trying to get the youngest dressed. The little boy was the same age as my little brother.

The next oldest boy, who was younger than me, came to the door and asked what I wanted. I said I wanted to play. He asked his mom and she smiled and said sure. So he and his next older brother came outside to play with me. I had brought a doll with me and they thought that was so funny. I said we could play on Joanie's swing, so we did. (That swing didn't last long because the boy's dad replaced it with a really big, fun rope swing that we would spend hours playing on. We would swing round and round underneath the huge weeping willow tree.)

Those boys became my playmates and I became a tom-boy! I still liked to play with dolls and have tea parties when I was with other girls. But when I was with the boys, I wanted to do boy things! Those brothers seemed to be only about a year apart from each other, but only two really became my playmates. One was my about my age and the other a year younger. Since I was so small and seemed younger than my years, we got along famously.

The first summer the tribe lived next door, I learned to do so many things. Now that I was a tom-boy, I could climb trees (a passion I lived for), play baseball, kick-the-can, and help build a tree house. I was five years old and should have been looking forward to going to kindergarten. But the local newspaper said there would be no Kindergarten that year. I was disappointed because my older brothers had told me how fun it was. Oh well, I had my newfound friends to play with and no kindergarten meant more time to play and have adventures. Those boys certainly knew how to find adventure!

The grass in the big field was very tall. We decided it looked just like Africa and we were going on a Safari. We got our lunch, our sticks (which had magically changed into machetes), and wore old dish towels over our heads, under our hats to keep the sun off our necks. I didn't know how those boys knew about Safari's, but I was a quick learner, and did my best to make them glad I was their playmate. We took off into parts unknown and hiked through the tall grass, looking for lions, tigers, elephants, snakes, and whatever other animals came to mind. We had an exciting day of hunting (when the machetes conveniently turned into rifles) and we narrowly escaped being caught and eaten by cannibals!

One day the tribe actually began to really look like Indians. (Back then we referred to Native Americans as Indians. There was no harm intended; that's just the way it was.) The boys were outside in the area where we played baseball. Their dad had a chair out there and a long extension cord hooked up to electric clippers. He had the boys, one by one, sit in the chair while he shaved their heads! He completely removed all the hair from the sides of their heads, all the way to the back. He left a strip of hair from the front top of their scalp all the way to the base of their skulls. They looked like Indians, just like the pictures in some of our books. He told them that their haircuts were called Mohawks, like the Indians, and asked me if I wanted mine cut too.

I declined and was thankful for the moment that I was a girl. He put the barber equipment away and we had a good game of kick-the-can. Other boys in the neighborhood came to play, but no other girls showed up. That was okay with me. I was enjoying playing with the boys, and really didn't miss playing with dolls. I didn't even miss Joanie. I never forgot her; I wonder if she remembers me.

CHAPTER 17

Alice

MY FIRST MEMORY of Alice was when mom took me and my brothers down to the house where I had the mishap with the cow pie. My older brothers hung out with the two boys that lived there; they were really good buddies. (We had been neighbors before we moved into the Big House.) Alice was there visiting. I knew her because I wasn't afraid of her at all; yet, I have no recollection of her before that particular day. She asked my mom if she could take me out in her boat. Mom said, "Yes."

I had never been in a row boat before; I was really excited! Alice had me put on a bumpy, orange vest that she called a life jacket. It was very rough where it touched my skin. I was glad I was fully clothed, because that vest would really have scratched me something awful! She had me take my shoes and socks off, and leave them on the dock. She said it's always best to have bare feet in a boat or on the dock, because if you fall in, you can swim better with bare feet.

Alice helped me into the boat and told me to sit on the back seat (it looked more like a bench to me). She pushed off from the dock and climbed into the boat in one swift move; I don't know how she did it! The oars were laying inside the boat. She lifted each one, and put the long piece of metal that protruded from a ring around each oar into a hole on each side of the boat. Next, she used one oar to turn us out to the open water (Hidden Cove wasn't really very open). We were on our way!

Alice showed me how to row, and I got to sit beside her and help; it was fun. I loved to watch the whirlpools that formed each time the oar pulled through the water. Sometimes, I would row too shallow and the water would splash;

sometimes too deep, and I could hardly move the oar. (I think Alice was letting me make mistakes so I could learn what worked and what didn't.) After a while, she had me sit back on the rear seat so I could see the scenery.

We rowed all the way around a little island that had a small cabin on it. It looked like someone lived in the cabin. I couldn't figure out how they could go anywhere unless they had a boat and I didn't see one anywhere. I asked Alice, and she said he was probably out fishing. We rowed underneath trees that hung over the salt water. One of them had a rope swing hanging so close to the water I could reach out and touch it. I wanted to swing on that swing above the water; it looked so fun!

Suddenly a fish jumped out of the water! It was very silver in the late afternoon sun. Alice stopped rowing and said to listen very carefully. I could hear insects humming. We watched, and pretty soon there were little fish jumping all over the water! They were trying to catch the mosquitoes or insects flying just above the water.

My mother's call stopped our fun adventure. She was standing on the beach in front of her friend's house waiting for me to come back so we could go home. I was so sad; I couldn't bear to leave my friend Alice and her wonderful row boat. I know I got tears in my eyes even though I was trying to be big and not cry. Alice said I could come again real soon and that we would go swimming before our boat ride. I told her I didn't know how to swim and she said she would teach me!

I could not stop talking the whole way home. I loved the boat, the water, Alice, and she was going to teach me to swim! Mom said that's nice and not much else. I really didn't give her a chance; I was so full of words, trying my best to express to Mom how much I loved the water and Alice. (Looking back I think my mother was a little jealous.)

Several days went by before we went back to my mom's friend's house. I had my swimming suit on, and I was really excited to learn to swim. I had played in the water many times, but no one had ever taught me to swim. I just thought Alice would show me how and I would do it. How hard could it be? I was in for quite a surprise!

Alice was waiting for me at Mom's friend's house. We left the two of them with their cups of coffee and my little brother, while we walked along the beach to Alice's house. We set my towel and clothes down on the lawn and walked out on the muddy beach.

The mud squished between my toes; it was really nasty. The first thing we did was walk out in the water to my knees and get down on all fours. Then Alice told me to use my hands like feet, and walk them on the bottom. She instructed me to stretch my legs out behind me while I kicked my feet. That sounded easy enough; she showed me how to do it. The soft, muddy bottom oozed up between my fingers. Yuck! There were sharp pieces of broken shells and barnacles in that gooey mud. I cut my fingers several times. Alice said the salt water would clean them off and not to worry.

We walked with our hands, kicking our feet, back and forth in front of her house. After I was confident with that task, she showed me how to blow bubbles. Now this was fun and easy; I did this all the time in the bath tub. We kicked and blew and got our faces all the way in the water. I thought swimming was great fun. Then Alice said to stand up.

Alice picked me up and carried me out to deeper water; it was up to her waist. She started to set me down, but my feet couldn't touch the bottom. I panicked and held onto her for dear life! She just laughed and said there was nothing to worry about; the deeper the water, the easier it is to float. Did she really think I would believe that? I was not about to let go!

Alice promised to hang onto me while I just practiced blowing bubbles and kicking my feet in the deep water. As long as Alice was holding onto me, I was okay. I didn't want her to let go, but at the same time, I didn't want her to think I was a baby. This was a terrible situation for a little girl like me! I just kept up the appearance of bravery and did the best I could. All of a sudden, she said that was enough of that, and turned me over onto my back!

"Oh my goodness," I exclaimed, "the water is in my ears!"

Alice thought nothing of that and said it would just clean the wax out of my ears. I had suffered through many earaches by that time in my life, and I did not like the feeling of water in my ears. I was terrified of getting an earache! Alice wanted me to let my head be way down in the water so my ears were underneath. She said if my head was down and my bottom was up, I would float all by myself. She told me to relax, and that she would keep her hand under my back. I thought

I might as well give it a try, maybe this whole ordeal would get over sooner. I closed my eyes and let my head go back so my chin was up. I pushed my bottom toward the surface of the water. (I could feel Alice's hand beneath my back.) I took a big breath of air and slowly let it out; Alice's hand was gone. I was floating on the water all by myself!

I don't know why I thought I needed to tell Alice I was floating, but I did. She said she knew it, and she was so proud of me. All of a sudden, she scooped me up into her arms and said that was enough for today! I was cold, covered in goose bumps, and shivering. Alice carried me to the shallow water and put me down. She said if I laid down in the shallow water, I would warm up. She was right. The water was really warm and so was the gooey mud.

We laid there for a while, and then got up and ran across her lawn to the hose. The hose had been laying in the afternoon sun and she let me rinse off first. That water felt hot; but it also felt really good. Alice rinsed off and we went into her house to put on our clothes. That was the first time I was ever in Alice's house. It was way different from any house I had ever been in. The furniture was all made from wood and canvas, like tents are made of. She even had a hammock in her living room! She must have noticed my wonder and awe, because she said, "I love the water and the beach and everything about them. So I live inside just as if I were out there." She pointed out the window to the water.

We walked back to my mom's friend's house. I was so excited. I could kick and blow bubbles with my face in the salt water. I could float on my back. But the very best thing was that I loved the water, and the beach, and everything about them!

CHAPTER 18

Trail to the Beach

I NOW LOVED the beach, the salt water, and all the possibilities for fun that environment promised. I could see the water from my bedroom window and often I would gaze at the inviting, blue water as it sparkled in the sunlight. It looked like it was just below the Tribe's field from my perspective. There was a trail going down to the beach, between our backyard and the Tribe's field. I had never been allowed to go down that trail until now.

The Tribe's father was taking the boys on an adventure and I was invited! We met just outside the place where the old, wooden gate created the passageway into the Tribe's field. Only this time, instead of walking on the trail through the field to the Tribe's house, we formed a single file line behind the Tribe's dad, and headed down the trail that led to the beach!

On our right hand side (which was our property) was a huge thicket of blackberries. They were plump and ripe, just beckoning us to have a bite. The dad was helping himself to handfuls, and soon the boys began to indulge. I was a little more timid about putting my hands into the thicket that was covered with stickers and bees, not just ripe berries. But their teasing made me overcome my fear, and I reached in to pluck a very plump berry. I popped it into my mouth and bit down. The sweet juice permeated every nook and cranny of my mouth. Yum! I gulped down a handful in record time.

Soon, however, the tribe's dad said we had enough and we better get going before the tide came in. What on earth was a tide? Where was it coming in from? Oh well, who cared, we were going to the beach. At the far corner of the Tribe's field, but on the trail side of their fence, was where the beach trail changed from a grassy-covered, straight path to a dirt, foot trail. The trail proceeded down the hill in a big, zigzag pattern. We stood at the top, gazing down the steep hill, onto a wonderful trail that went to the right, then to the left, and back again four times! It reminded me of a ride at the fair, only instead of sitting in a chair that had a bar across us, we were free to walk, or run, and swing our arms. How good could life be?

The walking part of the trail was very solid beneath our feet, but only wide enough for single file. (I always ended up at the back of these hikes. I don't know if it was because I was a girl, or because I was slower than the boys. Perhaps a little of both.) Down the trail we proceeded as the Tribe's dad admonished us to stay on the path, and not to slide down the steep hills in between the zigs and the zags. He said it was for our safety, but as I think back, I'm sure it was to help maintain the pathway. (I later learned that the pathway was owned by the people who owned the beach house at the base of the trail.)

We arrived at the end of the trail, and ended up in the back yard (if you could call it that) of a little beach house. No one was home, so we walked around to the front of the house, and stood on the deck overlooking the beach and the water. The beach was mostly covered in rocks, some of which, held many barnacles. There were a few patches of sand and some other areas that were slippery clay! The clay felt just like the clay Mom gave me to play with. I was amazed it was there on the beach and wondered how it had gotten there. We bought clay from the store.

The water was very cold! It was not like the water at Alice's beach. I didn't think swimming in this water would be as much fun as the warm water at Alice's. But swimming was not on the agenda the Tribe's dad had planned. He had this day planned really well. (Looking back I realize what an amazing father he was to those boys. He kept them so busy, they had no time for trouble, and he was able to teach them so much while they just thought they were playing or having an adventure. I was so blessed to have the Tribe next door.) He led us on a hike down the beach to the south, and told us not to go further than the big rock when an adult wasn't with us. He took us north, and said never to go past the bend of the beach when an adult wasn't with us. He also said to never come down to the beach alone. We had to always have at least a group of three. If one of us got hurt or in some sort of danger, someone could run for help while the other one stayed to keep an eye out.

We learned about the incoming tide. It was the water! Every day the tide would come in and go out twice. When the tide was coming in, it was safe to play and swim in the water. When the tide was going out, it was really best to not go into the water. There was a very strong current during an outgoing tide, and the water could quickly pull a grown person under the water and north to Agate Passage. The area underneath the Agate Pass Bridge was a narrow water-way called Agate Passage. Bainbridge Island was linked to the mainland via that bridge. The water through the passage moved swiftly and it was very dangerous.

The Tribe's dad said it was time to start for home. We had to climb the zigzagged trail up the hill this time. It was much harder than going down. We pretended we were mountain climbers and had great fun all the way up through the woods. We were reminded to stay on the foot path and not to take a short cut up the steep bank, even if we were sure we could do it. We had to help take care of the trail.

Once up onto the grassy path, we headed straight to the blackberries! After that long day, we were hungry and thirsty; those berries were just the refresh-ment we needed. We over-indulged, I'm sure, because I wasn't hungry for dinner that night. Mom couldn't understand how I could be out hiking all day and play-ing with the boys and not be hungry. I told her about the berries, and she said she had a job for me to do in the morning. I went to bed that night full of happy thoughts. I had a beach with a really neat trail down to it. And, I had blackber-ries; tons of them!

CHAPTER 19

Blackberries

MY MARVELOUS DISCOVERY of the previous day, had opened my mother's eyes to endless possibilities of wonderful food for her family; and it was free! Immediately after breakfast, Mom gave me a metal bowl, and told me to fill it with ripe blackberries. She told me not to eat very many because the bowl would get full much faster if I didn't waste time eating them. She also informed me that she would make blackberry pie for dessert that night!

I wasted no time in going out to the huge berry thicket and starting my morning work. I had hardly begun, when most of the Tribe next door showed up. They each had a pan or can, anything that would hold berries, and they were there for the very same reason as me. I felt threatened. There was only one of me and four of them! I picked as fast as I could. They were eating a lot of the berries, so I tried to not eat so many and get my bowl filled faster. I scurried into the house, got another large bowl, and went back out to pick more. I wasn't going to let those boys pick all of MY berries! As the Tribe members filled their bowls, in turn they would go back to their house and come back with an empty container. They were picking a lot more berries than I was. It seemed unfair, even to some-one as young as I was.

When my second bowl was full, I brought it back into our big kitchen. Mom was so happy with those berries and with me. I told her about the boys and she said not to worry. She rinsed the berries in the kitchen sink. The sink got a large purple stain on it and mom had to scrub it with some smelly powder that made it hard for me to breathe. I coughed a lot and she seemed worried and had me drink some water with lemon in it. It was sour, but I liked it.

Mom made blackberry pies. She let me help by rolling the dough out on the floured bread board. She sprinkled flour on the board and put a big hand full of dough on the board. Next, she put flour onto the rolling pin and sprinkled some on top of the mound of dough. Then I got to roll the dough. I rolled in one direction a few times, then Mom would sprinkle some more flour on the flat dough, and I would roll in another direction. I told Mom that I wanted to sprinkle the four too, so she let me. I rolled the dough until it was thin and bigger than the pie pan. Mom peeled the dough off the wooden board, and put it into the bottom of a pie pan; then I rolled out another mound of dough. When the next pie pan had a crust in the bottom, Mom filled the two pies with berries. She had mixed in some sugar and flour and it was very juicy! Mom then had me roll out two more mounds of dough, which she in turn, placed on top of the pies. Then I watched as Mom sealed the edges together by what she called, "Fluting."

Mom used a fork and made a big B on one of the pies. I didn't go to Kindergarten but I knew the letter B. I asked if I could do the other one and she let me. She said B was for berry. I said we could have two B's for blackberry and she agreed. I was having a good time practicing my B's and helping bake blackberry pies. But, the yummy treats had only just begun! Mom said to go and pick some more berries, and this time she got my older brothers to help.

We were a force to be reckoned with! Sure, there were four Tribe members from next door picking berries and only three of us. But my oldest brother was older and bigger than any of those boys, and he could reach the big berries that were up higher! The race was on! We picked as fast our fingers could move, being careful not to squish the juicy berries. Our bowls filled up quickly, and we hurried into the big kitchen, proud to show Mom our accomplishment. She was elated, and promised that we would be happy that we had worked so hard.

She was right. Mom made us pies, cobblers, shortcakes, jam, jelly, and lots of fresh blackberries with cream. Every day we would pick berries in the morning before it got too hot, and Mom would make something wonderful for us to eat. I was sad when the berries were all gone; picking them wasn't very fun, but I sure liked eating blackberry pie.

CHAPTER 20

Tunnels in the Attic

ANOTHER ONE OF the great discoveries of that summer were the tunnels in the attic. My older brothers were the ones who made the astonishing discovery. They immediately showed the two oldest Tribe members, who then let their younger brothers and me in on the secret.

Upstairs, from one end of our big house to the other, were two hidden tunnels on either side of the house. In my bedroom, and at the other end of the house in Jerry's room, were two attic closets on each side of the rooms. Those closets on each side were connected to the closets on each side at the other end of the house. Let me explain. In my room, on the south end of the house, I had an attic closet on the east side and on the west side. From either one of those closets, I could crawl through the tunnel to the closet in my brother's room at the opposite end. There were four attic closets and two wonderful tunnels. How lucky could kids be?

Those tunnels gave us endless hours of fun and adventure. We were always very quiet in a tunnel, and never let my little brother know where we were. The littlest Tribe boy wasn't allowed to know either. (I don't remember if they ever played in the tunnels when they got older.) We didn't tell Mom and Dad; somehow we knew, it was better to keep it a secret.

During the summer, we spent most of our time playing outdoors. It seemed like there was a lot more sunny weather when we were small children. Likewise, during the winter, we had more days of snow. Of course, at this time in our lives, we didn't know anything about changing weather patterns; we just knew that sunny days were meant to be enjoyed outside and rainy days were meant for the tunnels!

At first we used flashlights to see where we needed to place our hands between the joists that crossed the tunnel floor every two feet or so. It was not long afterwards, that we were comfortable just feeling our way through the long, tunnel. We always remembered that the roof sloped above us, all the way to the floor of the tunnel, so we needed to be sure to not try and stand up in the dark! There was absolutely no light in those tunnels. They were certainly no place to be if you were afraid of the dark!

One of my greatest joys was bringing my young girl friends on an adventure through a tunnel. I had several very good friends during my early years; girls that were as close to me as a sister. It was not until I was school age, that the invitations to tunnel expeditions began to be a ritual. But even at that early age, the joy of adventure and the pride of ownership gave me a great feeling of satisfaction. I had tunnels in the attic and my friends didn't.

After a few years, Mom found out when my little brother started crying because he wanted to go into the tunnel but was afraid. He told Mom and she told Dad, and Dad blocked the entrances to the best play area in our big, old house!

CHAPTER 21

Aunt Helen and Uncle Alex

AUNT HELEN AND Uncle Alex came to visit when I was five years old. Aunt Helen sounded like my other aunts, who were my dad's sisters. But, Uncle Alex talked funny! He said it was his Hungarian accent. My mom told me that even though Uncle Alex was born in the United States, his parents and family members all had Hungarian accents, so he learned to speak their way. I loved to hear Uncle Alex talk; he made me smile. He was very handsome too. He had black hair and a golden suntan. (Even at that early age, I knew a handsome man when I saw one!)

Aunt Helen seemed to want to spend time with me. I liked being the center of attention, so I decided to take advantage of the situation and asked her if she would push me on my swing. She informed me I needed to say, "Please."

"Hey, would you please push me on my swing?"

"My name isn't hay! It's Aunt Helen."

"Aunt Helen, would you please push me on my swing?"

"Yes, I would be delighted."

I guess Aunt Helen wanted me to be a proper lady and use proper English. That was fine with me; I had her all to myself and I was enjoying our time spent together. I enjoyed it until a Robin flew in front of me as I was swinging forward and pooped on my white blouse! Yuck! It was wet and sort of blue and white. Aunt Helen said it was blue from eating blackberries. (At least the Robin knew what tasted good.) She said to hurry into the house and rinse my blouse in cold water so it wouldn't get a stain. Aunt Helen was very smart and knew lots of things just like my mom.

During the long afternoons, Mom and Uncle Alex would look at old photographs and talk about when Mom was young. It was hard for me to imagine my mother as a little girl. It seemed to me that she had always been old. I knew that Uncle Alex was older than my mom, but he didn't look any older than her. I wondered how old he and Aunt Helen were. Curious as I was, I was too polite to ask.

Looking at all those old photographs must have brought back many childhood memories for my mother. One night she and my Uncle sang a song in Hungarian. My mother couldn't remember all of the words, but Uncle Alex knew it really well. They sounded really pretty together. My mother had a pretty voice; she was a very talented person. I always knew that; she was such a good artist and could make all kinds of neat things. She never sang very much, but when her Uncle was there, she just couldn't help herself.

I guess mom and Uncle Alex were making plans for when my Grandma and Grandpa Alviti were going to come. Grandma Alviti and Uncle Alex were brother and sister. Grandma and Grandpa were coming any day and preparations were underway. Mom was doing a lot of cooking, Uncle Alex was going down to the beach to fish, Aunt Helen was cleaning and ironing. My brothers and I (even my little brother) were busy playing with the Tribe and other kids from the neighborhood. My oldest brother had lots of friends around Seabold, and he was allowed to walk far from home. My brother Warren had lots friends too, but his were a little closer to home. My friends were either right next door or only a few doors away. It was really helpful to my mom for all of us children to be out of the house and let the grown-ups work.

Finally, one evening after dinner, Mom said that Grandma and Grandpa would be there tomorrow. Aunt Helen and Uncle Alex must have known because they were not surprised. I wished my dad could be there too, but he was fishing in Alaska. I wondered if Grandma and Grandpa talked like Uncle Alex. I could hardly sleep that night I was so excited.

CHAPTER 22

The Haircut

GRANDMA AND GRANDPA didn't arrive until the early afternoon. It was after lunch time, but still far from time for dinner. They must have been hungry because Mom and Aunt Helen made coffee and brought out all sorts of sandwich fixings, fruit, and sweet breads. The grown-ups sat around the big, dining room table and ate while they talked and laughed, and even cried. It must have been a very happy time for them; I was just busy staring at Grandma and Grandpa and listening to them talk. They both talked funny, but different from each other. Grandma and Uncle Alex talked the same; Grandpa talked really different.

Grandpa was a barber. He made money by cutting people's hair. I think he only cut men and boys' hair, but he kept looking at mine. Grandma was looking at my hair too. I'm sure it looked a mess. Mom seldom had time to fix my long hair into curls or braids or even a pony tail. It was blonde, long, and very stringy according to Grandma. Grandma decided that she needed to cut my hair. I didn't think that was a good idea; I liked my hair just the way it was.

That night after dinner, instead of cutting my hair, Grandma, Uncle Alex and Aunt Helen, and my mom had a dance. They put on colorful clothes from Hungary and danced to music playing on a record. They laughed and sang along and danced folk dances from the land where Grandma was born. Grandpa was in charge of the phonograph and placing the needle onto the record. He would do it without making a scratching sound. He clapped his hands to the music and had just as much fun as the dancers. My older brothers were at their friend's houses and I and my little brother watched the festivities with keen interest. I wanted to be a Hungarian too!

The next day was the day I was dreading. Grandma was going to cut off my hair! She had me sit on my red, high stool and she draped a sheet over me, covering my whole body except for my head. She pinned the sheet at the back of my neck with a diaper pin. She had set up the chair in the dining room, so I could see my reflection in the large mirror hanging on the far wall.

My hair hung down to the middle of my back. She brushed my hair to get rid of all the tangles. Then she gathered it all into her one hand and cut it off in one swift cut! All of a sudden, my hair was barely to my shoulders. Next she cut my bangs. That process was more difficult and took a lot more time. I was getting tired of sitting on my stool. I started to complain, and she told me to be quiet; she would be done in a few minutes. She trimmed and combed, cut and brushed. By the time she was finished, my hair barely covered my neck!

Grandma had me sweep my hair into the dust pan and throw it in the garbage. That was the last time my hair was ever down to the middle of my back. It would grow out a little longer, sometimes long enough for short braids, pigtails, or even a ponytail, but never again down my back. That was okay. (As the years went by, I liked my hair short and seldom would let it grow very long. Isn't it interesting how something so insignificant can be so life changing?)

CHAPTER 23

Plum Dumplings

GRANDMA WAS A good cook, just like my mom. She was busy during most of her visit just cooking. Aunt Helen spent a lot of time cleaning before she and Uncle Alex left. Grandma and Grandpa stayed a few more days. Grandpa read the newspaper, went for walks, and fished. Grandma cooked. She wanted our cupboards full of her baking. (Our food cupboards were different than in our homes of later years. These cupboards were extra cool inside. They had vents going to the outside of the house on the east side so the air was always cool. There were screens for the shelves instead of wood. Somehow, it kept food cool and it lasted longer.) Grandma spent hours cooking and filling those cupboards.

We had a lot of plum trees in our back yard, in addition to the peach tree, and the many apple trees. Grandma said she was going to make plum dumplings for dessert. I couldn't imagine what a plum dumpling was, but it sounded really delicious. If those sweet plums were part of the delicacy, then plum dumplings had to be one of the best desserts ever! My brothers and I were very happy to go and fill a bucket with plums.

We would climb the plum trees and shake the branches so the plums would fall to the ground. Then we would climb down and gather up the fallen plums. It didn't matter if they were split or had some skin missing because they were going to be cooked in the plum dumplings. We were in a hurry to see and taste what plum dumplings were. We rushed back into the big kitchen with the bucket almost overflowing.

Grandma dumped the plums into the kitchen sink and washed them under the running water. We had a faucet in our kitchen sink instead of a pump like at our other grandma's house. (A faucet made kitchen work a lot faster and easier.) Grandma then had us take turns, each removing pits from the plums by breaking them open where the crease was. My oldest brother could do it really well; mine were torn and messy.

While we were doing that task, Grandma was making dough. She rolled the dough into a large square and then cut the big square into smaller squares. She placed a plum at one corner, sprinkled some raisins, sugar, and cinnamon on each plum and rolled the plum up into the dough square, turning in the corners as she rolled. We hadn't noticed, but while we were pitting the plums, Grandma had also made a large kettle of syrup and it was heating on the stove. She dropped the dough-covered plums one by one into that hot, boiling syrup and they began to cook. After a few minutes, she lowered the heat on the stove and put the lid on the pot. The sweet, spicy smell permeated the kitchen, then the whole house.

I was sitting in the corner on my red, high-stool enjoying the smell of the simmering dumplings. When I tried to slide down off the stool to help Grandma, my foot got tangled in the bar near the lower part of the stool's legs. I tripped and fell against the corner of the counter top by the sink. There was a strip of metal along the edge of the counter top and the corner was very sharp. As I fell, the corner caught the left side of my upper lip and sliced it open! Grandma grabbed a kitchen towel and covered my mouth so fast I hardly knew what had happened. She called for Grandpa to come into the kitchen and look at my mouth. He made a butterfly out of adhesive tape and taped it closed. I was very upset and my lip hurt terribly, but I wasn't going to let that mishap spoil the plum dumplings I was waiting for.

I cannot remember what we ate for dinner that night. All I can remember is eating plum dumplings covered with fresh cream. Oh what a delightful treat that was. Grandma came to visit every summer for about three years and made plum dumplings every time. (My mother never made them and neither have I.)

CHAPTER 24

Puss and Boots

WE HAD A cat named Puss and a dog named Boots. They belonged to my brother Warren. However, for all practical purposes, they were the family pets. (I remember very little about them, but I love animals as I'm sure most of my readers do too. I will share what little I do recall.)

Puss was a black and white cat with medium length hair. Mom used to say she was a Tuxedo cat because of her coloring. She had white whiskers on a black face, a white chest and stomach, white paws, and a white tip on her tail. I knew she wasn't a very cuddly kitty because she always ran away when I wanted to pet or hold her. Mom said she was a good mouser.

Boots was a very friendly dog. She had black, wavy hair and a little white on her paws. I don't know what breed she was, probably a Heinz 57. I remember how loyal she was to my brothers. When they walked to the school bus stop in the morning, she went with them. She came home after they got on the bus and waited on the front porch all day. When it was close to the time their bus should be coming, she walked to the bus stop to greet them and walk them home. She was a very good dog!

After several months, Boots began staying away all day while my brothers were at school. When they came home, she was with them. She stayed home the rest of the day and all the night until she walked with them to the bus stop the next morning. We didn't see her again until the boys came home. My mother started asking people if they knew where Boots was during the day.

Mr. Carlson, the store keeper where the bus stopped, said he saw Boots every morning and afternoon with the boys but he didn't see her during the day.

Mom went to the houses of the people who lived near the bus stop. Sure enough, Mom found Boots at one of the houses. The lady who lived there said Boots just came over one day after the bus left and stayed on her door step all day until the bus brought the kids back in the afternoon. She left with the boys and came back the next morning. She said that Boots was such a nice dog that she let her stay.

We shared Boots with that family for a couple of years. Then one day Boots did not come home. My brother went to their house looking for Boots and discovered that she had moved in with them! She just decided that she like them more than us! My brother was very sad about it. We were all a little sad, but realized that Boots liked it there better and they loved her. So we let Boots live with them for the rest of her life.

Puss continued to be our elusive family cat. She would leave her hunting conquests on the front or back door step almost every morning. Puss lived with us for a few years and then one day she was gone; she simply disappeared.

The house wasn't the same without a pet. We went through several cats and dogs without success. Something terrible happened to them all. Between being hit by cars and killed in unfortunate accidents (my mother stepped on the sofa when our orange kitty was inside under the springs and the kitty got squished), we had no success in having a family pet for a very long time.

CHAPTER 25

Halloween

HALLOWEEN WAS COMING and I was filled with anticipation. I was going to go trick-or-treating! My brothers told me wonderful stories about dressing up in costumes so no one recognized who you were. They said you carried a bag and went from house to house saying, "Trick-or-treat," and the grown-ups at each house would put goodies into your bag. This sounded like something really worth doing. The Tribe next door were very excited about it too. My little friends with whom I played were excited too. The bigger kids, Jerry's friends, were really excited. They kept teasing me and saying that the goblins were going to get me, but I knew they were just teasing. I had seen the ghost in our house and I knew he wouldn't hurt anyone.

My dad was home from Alaska and he seemed very happy about all the excitement. He was helping Mom make our costumes. He wouldn't sew or anything like that, but he would buy her things she said she needed from the store. I was going to be a fairy princess. Mom found me a beautiful dress at the rummage sale and cut and sewed on it till it fit perfectly. She made me a wand with a sparkling star on the end. My mother could do anything!

The day of Halloween our costumes were ready, and Mom spent the day cooking. We got to help by unwrapping caramel candies and dropping them into a large pot. She heated the caramels until the whole bunch was a thick mass of gooey syrup. Next, she stuck little wooden sticks into the end of each apple and dipped them into the caramel syrup and swirled them around. She pulled them out and set them in paper cupcake liners that she had us spread open; they sure looked good.

Mom also baked lots of chocolate chip cookies. Chocolate chip cookies were my favorite kind of cookie. My Aunt Virginia made really good chocolate chip cookies, but they were thick like scones. Mom's cookies were thin and the chocolate pieces stuck out from them. I would always take the cookies that had the most chocolate candy protruding from the crunchy cookie. Yum! Life was so good.

Finally after a long day of cooking and trying to be patient, it was time to get on our costumes. Mom put a little crown on my head, so I would look pretty. It was hard to look like a fairy princess with my hair cut short. (Even at my young age, I knew I should have my hair in a bun!) I can't remember what my brothers wore that year; it was such a long time ago. But I do remember trick-or-treating.

Dad helped us into the Pontiac and we drove to different neighbors' houses. He would stop the car and we would climb out. I had to straighten my dress every time I climbed out of the car. My brothers always got to the door and knocked before I was half-way there. I kept missing out on saying trick-or-treat. At one house, the lady told me I couldn't reach into the big bowl until I said the magic words. Even I knew the magic words were "Please" and "Thank you." I said, "Please," and she laughed! She told me that tonight the magic words were trick-or-treat and I needed to say them before she could give me anything. I said, "Trick-or treat," and she let me grab a big candy bar, a cupcake, and a box of Cracker Jacks. I remembered to say, "Thank you," and we were on our way back to the car and the next house. My brothers said that was the best house in the neighborhood to trick-or-treat at because they didn't have kids and liked kids a lot!

After visiting the homes of everyone in our neighborhood, we drove to our aunts and uncles homes. We got more yummy things to put into our bags. Sometimes, we would see our cousins dressed up in their costumes; sometimes they didn't have a costume on and they were the ones passing out the treats!

By the time we went home that night, I was exhausted. Mom had saved us each a caramel apple, but the chocolate chip cookies were all gone. It didn't even matter because our bags were full of cookies, candy, Cracker Jacks, cupcakes, apples, oranges, and packages of chewing gum. Life was good!

CHAPTER 26

The Hospital Again

I WAS SICK again. That seemed to be a routine part of my young life. I was always getting sick with something. Mom was always worrying about me, and talking about me to my aunts and uncles. I could hear her on the phone this particular day. She was telling my Aunt Jessie that I needed to go to the hospital and could she please watch my little brother. I really couldn't understand why I needed to go to the hospital; I didn't feel any worse than I ever felt when I didn't feel good.

Of course my objections and arguments fell upon deaf ears. Away, to the ferry boat in Winslow, we went. Dad drove us and let us off in front of the terminal. Mom was carrying a suit case, that made me nervous. We went into the big building where Mom paid for her ticket. I was allowed to ride the ferry for free because I was a young child. I could read my numbers and some letters and I knew that the sign said something about 5 and under could ride for free. I really looked forward to turning 6 years old and having to pay to ride the ferry boat.

Mom got a man in a uniform to push me in a wheel chair down the long walkway to the ferry boat. There was a ramp between the walkway and the boat and he pushed down on the back of the wheelchair and the front went up and onto the ramp. He then wheeled me across the ramp and gently lowered me onto the deck of the ferry boat. He pushed me all the way to a seat inside by one of the big windows. I got out of the chair and Mom told him thank you. Mom told me to say thank you and I did. I was thinking I could have walked down the walkway by myself instead of causing all those people to stare at me.

When we arrived in Seattle, we walked off the ferryboat with no wheel chair! (At least I didn't need to be embarrassed any more.) Mom stood at a pay phone and called a number that was posted on a sign near the phone. A few minutes later, someone in a uniform walked into where we were waiting and tipped his hat at Mom and said he would drive us to the hospital. (I was not happy about this situation.) We rode in the back seat. The cab driver and my Mom talked the whole time to the hospital. When he let us out, my mom paid him, and he said to me, "Get well soon."

I couldn't figure that out; I really didn't feel sick. I had no idea of what I was there for! I recognized the big waiting room with all the colorful paintings on the walls. I was getting a sick feeling in my stomach; bad memories were over-coming me. We went to the big desk and mom talked with the woman behind the desk. The woman behind the desk kept looking at me and smiling; I kept thinking she knew something I didn't. Pretty soon a nurse in a stripped uniform came into the waiting room pushing a little wheel chair. "Hop in," she said.

I was thinking at least it wasn't a crib on wheels. However, I was still upset that they thought I needed a wheel chair; I could walk just fine! We went to a little room where someone took blood from my fingers; that hurt a lot! I tried to be brave and the man put band aids on each finger he stuck. Then we went to my room. It was very different from the room with the iron lung.

This little room was on the other side of the hallway; far from the windows that looked over the city. The only window in the room faced the hallway. There was no other bed in the room; just the crib on wheels that I had to stay in. I was five years old and they thought I needed to be in a crib; life was terrible! There was a large leather chair beside my crib. Mom was told she could stay there, or out in the hall on the sofa, for the night. Mom stayed with me off and on through the night. She said the chair wasn't very comfortable. She told me several times that she was going to go have a cup of coffee or go smoke a cigarette. I certainly didn't get any sleep that night; in addition to all the noise from the hallway and Mom's fidgeting, I was extremely apprehensive about the coming day.

The day dawned all too soon and I had been right to be filled with appre-hension and foreboding. I was in for a horrible experience with no way to escape and no explanation of why they were doing this to me! The nurse came in to my room before I could even have any breakfast. She asked if I had to use the bathroom and then didn't even let me out of the bed. Instead she gave me one of those horrible bedpans and expected me to go with her watching. I told her I couldn't go with her watching and she said I was being silly. That was one battle I won; she left the room for a few minutes. She came back acting like I had been a bother and had made her late for something important. She cleaned me up, put a clean gown on me, and pushed me down the long hallway. I didn't even get a chance to see my mom!

The nurse left my crib in the hallway and went in through the door we had parked near. It seemed like I waited out there a very long time; I was getting very cold! (Even now, years later, I remember how cold I felt. I think it was mostly caused from nerves; I was very frightened.) All too soon the door opened, and the nurse came out and wheeled my crib into that cold, steel room. She let the side down from my crib and told me to climb out onto the table in front of me.

The table was cold, shining metal. What a horrible thing to tell a little girl to do! I did not want to do it and I was tired of trying to be brave. I started crying; throwing a tantrum was what they called it. They kept trying to stop me from crying by using their nice voices, but I wasn't going to cooperate. I had had enough! The nurse physically forced me to lie down on my left side. She held me down at my upper body and someone else held me down by leaning on my legs. I was crying and screaming to leave me alone. The doctor, who was sitting on a chair in front of me, acted upset and worried. He had been using his nice voice to try and calm me down; now he was silent and was definitely preoccupied.

Another nurse had a brown bottle and cotton balls. She washed my side, and part of my tummy and back with the brown liquid. It made me feel even colder than I already was. Then the nurse who was holding my upper body still said I was going to feel a sting, but to stay very still. The doctor, who was sitting in front of me, took the largest needle I had ever seen and stuck it into my side! I screamed and tried to roll away. The nurses held on to me as hard as they could. The doctor kept saying it would just be another minute. It seemed like many minutes to me; I wanted to escape but couldn't move!

Finally the ordeal was over. The needle was removed and a big bandage was put on my side. An ice-pack was put over that. I was so cold and I did not want the icepack, but they said I had to have it. They put lots of blankets on me and wheeled me back to that dark, little room. My mother was sitting in the leather chair waiting for me. She took one look at me and exclaimed, "Oh My God!"

I became hysterical again and cried very loudly. I wanted Mom to hold me and the nurse kept telling my mom that I needed to lay quietly in the bed for a while. Mom put her arm on me to comfort me and I fell asleep feeling safe and warm.

(Years later I figured out that I had had a biopsy from my liver. I had Gilbert's Syndrome and through the years it caused many misdiagnoses and undue worry and stress for my mother as well as me.)

CHAPTER 27

The Christmas Box

THIS WAS THE first of many Christmases that we received a Christmas box from Grandma and Grandpa Alviti. They had just visited us the past summer, so their memory was vivid in my mind. I remembered what a wonderful cook Grandma was. Mom said the box would be full of Grandma's cooking. Christmas was still a couple of weeks away, but we pestered my mother relentlessly until she gave in and let us open that box of sweet delights.

Grandma had outdone herself! The box was about two feet tall and wide, and was filled to the brim with all sorts of cookies and candy. Some of the cookies had broken during their travel to our house from California. We got to help Mom sort out the broken ones, and they went to a large plate so we could munch on them throughout the coming days. The ones that were still intact were set on pretty plates and covered with aluminum foil to wait for a special occasion. Some of the candy was put on the big plate with the broken cookies, but most of it got put into pretty dishes and put in the food cupboard for a another day. Many of the cookies were recipes from the old country; Mom told us that the old country was Hungary.

The box didn't have anything else in I, just lots of sweet things to eat. I guess Grandma thought sweet things were what kids loved best. I loved crayons and coloring books, clothes for Suzabella, Chinese Marbles, and Pick-Up Sticks. But, I guessed there was only room in the box for the yummy things Grandma sent.

We wanted to share our sweet treasure with the boys from the Tribe and our other friends. My mother was always saying we needed to save some for Christmas. But how do you tell young children to wait a week or longer before they get to eat something so yummy? We knew the goodies were in the cupboard and so did our friends. Whenever mom was in another room, busy doing whatever mothers do, we would snitch a few cookies or pieces of candy from one of the many plates or dishes in the cupboard. We would hold the delicacy in our hand, letting our hand fall at our side with the treasure hidden within our slightly curled fingers. We would walk right past Mom and she never knew our secret! Once up in our bedrooms or the playroom, we would share the little tidbits with whomever was visiting that day. The plates began to look like an army had marched through and hungry soldiers had attacked them. (My mother's words, not mine.)

When Christmas Eve came, Mom wanted to bring some of the cookies and candy to our Grandma's house in Seabold for dessert after the big dinner. Instead of a plate heaping with one type of cookie, she had to put a few of each kind onto one plate. She didn't complain, but I could see the disappointment on her face. I learned from that experience to not steal the cookies any more. I didn't like to make my mom unhappy; she had enough to deal with just being a mother to my two older brothers, me, and my little brother.

For the next seven years a box full of treats came at Christmas time. We learned to just eat the broken ones and save the pretty ones for special occasions. There were so many special occasions that we did not have to wait very long before we could close our mouths around those sweet delicacies from the old county.

CHAPTER 28

The Erector Set

CHRISTMAS EVE THAT year was every bit as wonderful as the year before. We got lots of presents and were filled with so much happiness, it's remarkable that we didn't explode! My brother Warren got the most amazing gift. I was just as intrigued by it as he and my oldest brother were. It was called an Erector Set. My little brother had no idea what it was and that was fine with us. We could hardly wait to begin construction!

The Erector Set was in a box. The set contained a huge assortment of metal building materials. They looked just like the steel beams and things we would see on the new construction at the soon to be IGA store in Winslow. In addition to the different size beams, there were all sorts of nuts, bolts, screws, and even wing nuts. There were lots of pictures of instructions on how to build different things. My brothers could read the instructions and understand the diagrams in the pictures. I couldn't; I just had to think what I wanted to build and then put it together.

I loved building with the Erector Set. I was very lucky to have a big brother who would let me play with it. I wasn't allowed to play when he was using it, and I wasn't allowed to take apart anything he had made. That was okay. He was gone to his friends' houses often enough that I had plenty of opportunity to create to my heart's content.

Building with the Erector Set gave me a new love, making things with my hands. I now loved playing with Tinker Toys and the plastic bricks that were red and white and came in different sizes. I never knew what they were called, but I sure enjoyed building houses, planes, cars, or anything I could think of.

My brothers got an electric train and all those building materials were put to good use creating the town where the train station was. I was fascinated by the train, the town, and everything miniature! Now my brothers' toys, such as Tinker Toys, plastic bricks, and even Jerry's wood burning kit had a new fascination. I had the ability to make things with my own two hands! I was just like my mother!

CHAPTER 29

Wonder Bread

ONE DAY MOM needed some bread to make us sandwiches for lunch. She was so busy she didn't have time to go to the store. She asked me if I would like to walk to the store and get a loaf of bread. She would give me some money and a note asking Mr. Carlson to fill the order. Then, I would carry the bag home and she could make our lunch.

Oh boy, this was a huge responsibility. I had never walked to the store by myself before. I had never been given money to buy bread for the family. I was really growing up! I was ready to go at that moment. Mom wrote a note to Mr. Carlson and gave me two dimes to carry in my pocket. I needed to wear my rain boots, a coat and hat, mittens, the works! It was still winter and cold outside. Mom reminded me that I would get Polio if I waded in the puddles. I was just supposed to walk right to the store, give Mr. Carlson the note, and he would get the loaf of bread and take my money. He would give me the change and I was supposed to bring home every cent along with the loaf of bread.

I took off, walking as fast as my little legs and feet could go. It wasn't really raining; just a light drizzle. I must have made it to the store in about 15 minutes. I climbed the three steps and pushed open the big door. Mr. Carlson was behind the big wooden counter. He smiled and asked where my mother was. I walked forward, feeling very important and reached into my pocket to retrieve the note. It wasn't there!

I reached into my other pocket and there were the two dimes. Whew! At least I didn't lose the money. I told Mr. Carlson that I was supposed to buy a loaf of bread. He asked me if my mother had sent me all that way by myself. I stood a little taller and smiled and answered, "Yes."

Mr. Carlson went over to his phone on the back wall. It was a huge, old black phone. It had a large hand piece that you listened in one end and spoke into the other end. There was a big, black box attached to the wall and the hand piece hung on a hook on the box. It was very different from our phone at home that sat on the desk. He called my mother to ask about me buying a loaf of bread. He said a few more words and thanked her and hung up.

Mr. Carlson walked down the aisle near the front windows. He picked up a loaf of Wonder Bread. I knew about Wonder Bread; it helped build strong bodies 12 ways! It was packaged in pretty plastic paper that had different size red and blue circles on the package. It looked wonderful to me. I told Mr. Carlson I only had twenty cents. He said that loaf of bread only cost nineteen cents. I said, "Okay."

Mr. Carlson sold me the loaf of Wonder Bread and gave me a penny to take home to my mother. I was so excited and hungry to eat some of that bread that could build strong bodies twelve ways! I carried the bag very carefully, so that I wouldn't squish the bread. I walked as fast as I could, switching the bag from one side to the other as I got tired of carrying it on one side. It never rained and I stayed warm and dry the whole way home. When I got home, there on the front porch steps was the note to Mr. Carlson!

I picked it up and went into the house. I showed Mom the note and gave her the penny. She was upset because I had bought expensive bread! She just wanted the plain white bread she always bought. It only costs fifteen cents and I had spent nineteen! She consoled herself with the fact that there were several more slices of bread in the loaf of Wonder Bread. And I reminded her that Wonder Bread builds strong bodies twelve ways!

CHAPTER 30

The Easter Egg Hunt

THE EASTER EGG Hunt at the Seabold Hall was so much fun. All of the children who attended the Sunday School at the Community Church were in attendance. I think there were a lot of other children there too! We had all dyed Easter eggs on Good Friday, and then our mothers' had brought the eggs in their cartons to the Hall. Someone had hidden all those dozens of eggs for us to hunt.

There were prizes awarded to the children who found the most eggs. I was never so lucky to find very many, but I had fun anyway. All the children were having a good time. I couldn't help but notice that the adults were having fun too! There were lots of cameras hanging from the necks of parents and people saying, "Smile."

There was the aromatic smell of coffee coming from the large kitchen in the Hall and the women had brought desserts to feed everyone. I hoped there was something with chocolate because anything chocolate was my favorite. I liked mincemeat too, but there was never anything made with mincemeat at Easter; it was always saved for Thanksgiving and Christmas.

Lots of times the weather on Easter was terrible; I had heard the adults say so. But this year, the weather was sunny and warm. I could be outside in just my dress and sweater. It was fun watching all the children scurrying to and fro with their baskets, searching for eggs hiding in the grass, in the bushes, near the bottoms of the trees, and anywhere else you could think of to look. On such a warm, spring day, we could have stayed out forever looking for those eggs. Someone found the golden egg and there were all sorts of cheers and clapping. After about half an hour, one of the adults suggested they count the eggs that had been found to see if we were about done with the Hunt. I didn't know what the hurry was; the weather was warm and I wanted to keep hunting.

(I didn't realize that the number of eggs were limited and they would run out at a certain point.) Soon a whistle blew and we were told the hunt was over. The kids of a certain age who had the most within their age groups won the prizes. The kid who found the golden egg got a special prize. I didn't win anything; I never did in future years either. But it didn't matter; we were going to have an egg hunt at Grandma's house after Easter dinner!

Dinner at Grandma's was just as busy and fun as at Christmas. My cousins, I rarely saw, where there too! I learned their names were Judy, Kenny, and Paul. On that Easter, I also learned that my other cousin, Neal (who I played Chinese checkers and Pick-Up Sticks with), was also their cousin. What a bunch of cousins! I was sure I was very lucky to have so many cousins. My little brother Davey wanted to be included with everything we, the older kids, were doing. It was annoying because we were five, almost six and he was only two!

We washed our hands in the kitchen sink with the pump. All of us children sat at the table in the kitchen for dinner; we weren't very hungry because we had already eaten some hard boiled eggs. However, there was a feeling of anticipation amongst us. The older cousins were eating dinner quickly so they could go out to the woods near Grandma's house and hide eggs for us to hunt. How lucky can little kids be to have two Easter egg hunts in one day?

Hunting eggs at Grandma's house was much more exciting than at the Community Hall. The woods with its cut wood piles, the gnarled tree stumps, and low growing bushes provided endless places to find eggs. We didn't get prizes and no one cared. We just had a lot of fun. We even discovered a horse tree!

CHAPTER 31

The Horse Tree

THE HORSE TREE, as we called it, was actually a Madrona Tree. It grew sideways near the base of the tree. It was a large tree and quite tall. However, near the base, it took a sideways stretch of about five or six feet before it straightened toward the ground. Hence, about three feet above the ground, there was a length of tree about as long as horse's back, that we could pretend to ride on. It was great fun. My cousin Neal, that I always played Chinese checkers and Pick-Up Sticks with, was the one who first introduced me to the Horse Tree.

That tree became a very important part of the ritual when we went to Grandma's house. Rain or shine, I always had to go for a quick ride on the Horse Tree. Sometimes the bark would peel. It felt like stiff paper and was scratchy. I could peel the bark off in very large pieces. When the bark came off, new bark grew back. My cousin could stand up on the tree and jump off. I was afraid to do that for a long time. There were short bushes growing near the tree and underneath the horse back part of the tree. I was afraid I couldn't jump far enough to clear the bushes. My cousin was a lot taller than I was. I was older than him and he was taller; sometimes life wasn't fair!

When I was a little older, I would bring my girlfriends to Grandma's house so they could ride the Horse Tree too. They thought it was just as much fun as I did. My little brother would cry because he wanted to ride the tree, but he was too heavy for me to pick up and put on the tree. When dad was home from Alaska, he would always take time to put my little brother on the tree. I can never remember any of the boys from the Tribe next door getting to ride on the Horse Tree. In fact, I can't remember any of the Tribe ever going to Grandma's house. I'm sure they must have, but I don't remember it; they were not relatives, just neighbors.

CHAPTER 32

Family Picnics

EVERY SUMMER, THE entire extended family that lived within a drive to the beach, gathered together on Sundays for a picnic. For years, the gathering took place at the Fay Bainbridge State Park, although I'm not even sure if during those early years it was a state park. There were some structures built up on the hill and on the beach for groups of people to gather in, protected from the wind and rain that so often accompanied us on the family picnics. There were other people, very close friends that joined us during the Sunday gatherings. Their children were the ages of us, so it made the gatherings even more fun.

There were swings up on the hill, monkey bars, and a very tall slide. The swings were the biggest I knew of; we could really swing high. The ground sloped down toward the beach in front of the swings, so it seemed like we were swinging far into the sky and back again. This particular summer I would turn six and my cousin Delores, who was much older than me, taught me how to pump myself on one of those big swings. It was so fun to be able to make myself swing without having to wait for someone to push me!

The slide was made from metal and someone always brought along a piece of waxed paper. The first person on the slide would sit on the paper and scoot themselves down, waxing the slide as they scooted along. The next person would use a fresh piece of paper if they had one, or reuse the already worn piece. The wax made the slide slippery and the second person got a faster, easier ride. By the third waxing, the slide reached perfection and we had a wonderful time. It was great exercise; we had to climb the tall ladder, slide down the slide, and then run around to the base of the ladder and do it all over again! Sometimes there was quite a long line of children waiting for their turn.

There were logs all along the area between the beach and the parking lot. Some were placed there on purpose, to divide the beach from the parking areas. Others were strewn haphazardly, piled on top of each other at odd angles. It was great fun to run along the logs, jumping from one to another, trying to never have to leave the logs and run in the sand beneath. We would have contests to see who could go the furthest without leaving the logs. Sometimes danger lurked in those logs. Several times there were loose logs and they would shift when weight was applied. Often the bark was loose and would peel off under the pressure of our feet getting too close to the side. That would usually end in falling off the log and scraping a knee or elbow. (The most frightening experience I ever encountered was when I was older and saw a large, black snake wiggle away from under the log I was walking on!)

When it was time to eat, we were ready. All that play and fresh salt air could really bring on an appetite! There was so much food, it was like going to a smorgasbord. There were salads, casseroles, hamburgers and hotdogs, desserts, and marshmallows to roast on a stick. My aunts were great cooks, just like my mom. The mothers of our friends must have been good cooks too because everything I tasted, I liked.

There was one exception; I don't know what possessed someone to think of bringing something so horrid to a picnic. The adults would talk about it for a long time and then act like they were eating the most remarkable delicacy. They called it lutefisk and looked like what flows out of a runny nose! It smelled like rotten fish and it tasted worse than that! I thought the grownups didn't have very good taste buds.

The Tribe began coming to our family picnics. They told us about a beach far up to the north past a place called Hansville. They said the beach was covered in sand, and you could walk far out into the water before it got deep. Plans were made to go to Twin Spits the next Sunday.

Twin Spits proved to be all the Tribe claimed. It was an amazing beach, like the ones I saw in books. The sand was hot, and when the tide would come in over the hot sand, it warmed the water. I got to practice my swimming, walking on my hands while kicking my feet. It was really nice to put my hands on the sand and not have gooey mud squishing between my fingers. I could doggy paddle for a few feet, but I would hold my breath with my face high out of the water. My mother realized something needed to be done about that.

When the wind blew, my uncles would pound driftwood into the sand and drape blankets, sheets, or tablecloths, anything that would block the wind. It also worked well to provide shade, since there were no trees or shelter of any kind out at Twin Spits.

From that first Sunday out at Twin Spits, our family picnics were spent on those soft, sandy beaches. We could gaze across the water at the Olympic Mountains. The water, the mountains, and the sky were all blended together in shades of blue. The Tribe had given all of us a wonderful gift, one that would last a lifetime.

CHAPTER 33

Swimming Lessons

MOM HAD DECIDED that I and the other kids needed swimming lessons. She made the arrangements for most of the kids in our neighborhood to take swimming lessons out at a place called Island Lake. I didn't know where Island Lake was, but it sounded like a really fun place. My oldest brother went to lots of parties out there with his friends.

On lesson day, my brother Warren, my little brother Davey, and I got on our swimming suits and put on our clothes over them. We got into the Pontiac and went to the Tribe's house and picked up all those boys. Then we picked up our cousins, Judy and Kenny, that lived a few houses further down the road toward Carlson's Store. We packed eleven kids into the car to go and take swimming lessons! Sometimes, I had to let someone else ride in my window seat; I wasn't happy about that. At least I didn't need to have someone sit on my lap; I was small so I always sat on someone else's lap. There was a rule in the Pontiac that no one could double up in the front seat. The two kids that got to ride up there were really lucky!

When we first got to the lake, we had to sign in or have Mom sign us in. Next we had to take a swimming test to show what we already knew how to do. Then we were divided into groups and assigned an instructor. (I always loved my instructors; they were forever smiling, very patient, and extremely encouraging. They taught me more than how to swim. They taught me how to teach other kids to swim, although I didn't know it at the time.)

The water in Island Lake was murky. We couldn't see our hands underneath the surface of the water. My instructor said that in the morning before anyone showed up for lessons, the water was clear. Then when more people began walking out into the water, it stirred up the bottom and the water became brown and yucky. She informed us that it wasn't a good idea for us to drink the water. I don't think any of us planned to drink the water, but it happened; it happened often!

We constantly had to keep putting our faces in the water and blowing bubble, even when we doggy paddled. Doggie paddling is exhausting work and really shouldn't be taught because of its inefficiency. But, it seems that children are naturally inclined to paddle like dogs when they first learn to swim; I was no different. I gulped mouthfuls of that dirty water and so did lots of other children! When lesson time was over, we got to play. You had to at least know how to doggie paddle in order to go down the big water slide.

The water slide was a big wooden slide that had a hose at the top with water running out the hose. It wet the metal sheet that lined the slide's surface. The wooden sides were not lined in metal, so we had to be careful to slide straight and not rub our bare skin against the wooden sides. Those sides were the cause of many splinters among many swimmers! The slide was quite steep, and we would practically fly down the slide, going faster the closer to the bottom we got. Near the bottom, the slope leveled off and turned slightly upward just before reaching the water. We would fly off the end of the slide, out about five or six feet, into water that was definitely over my head. I was glad I could doggie paddle and get back to where I could touch bottom. I really wanted to swim the way my instructor did; how long would it take me to learn?

It actually took me about three summers of going to lessons before I was swimming really well. I will always be grateful to my mother for being diligent enough to put up with all those kids, the noise, the complaining, and no doubt considerable money, to help all of us learn to swim.

CHAPTER 34

Jeweled Treasures

MY DAD HAD made me a wonderful sandbox. I loved to play in the sand, especially on a sunny day when the sand felt nice and warm. As I got older, I became more creative in my sandbox activities, and one day I had the brilliant idea to have a treasure hunt!

I had often played with the jewelry in the pretty box on the dresser in Mom's bedroom. She always let me try on the different necklaces, bracelets, earrings, etc. So I saw no problem with bringing the box of jewelry outside to the sand box. I simply went into her bedroom and grabbed the box and carried it outside to the back yard and into my sandbox. I then took the items, one by one, and buried them in the sand. Then I walked on the trail across the field to the Tribe's house and invited several of the boys to come for a treasure hunt.

They were only too happy to come on a treasure hunt! I was feeling quite pleased with myself because I had thought this great game up all on my own. I was giving the Tribe boys something exciting to play. They scurried into the sand box as soon as it was in sight.

They dug through the sand, finding sparkling treasures and putting them on or stuffing them into their pockets. One of the boys went and got their older brothers who brought some other kids over with them. When they had found all they could find, they went home and presented their mothers with beautiful presents. My mom got a phone call while I was still outside playing.

"Oh My God!" was all I heard while swinging on my little swing underneath the Crab apple tree. Mom came out onto the big porch and called down to me.

"Did you give away all my jewelry?" mom scolded.

"No, they had to find it," was my innocent reply. I knew from the sound of Mom's voice that I had done something wrong.

"You go and get every piece of it back right now!" Mom was really upset. I was embarrassed up one side and down the other! What would my friends think? I had told them they could keep whatever they found. Why was my mom being so unreasonable? Didn't she know the predicament she had put me in?

I went to the Tribe's house and to my cousins down the street. I went to my girlfriend's house and everywhere else I could think of. Some of my friends had given treasures to other friends, and it seemed to me, that everyone I knew of had some of mom's jewelry. That was a very long day!

I still remember my mother and her friends sitting at the dining room table drinking coffee and laughing over the day I gave away mom's jewelry. I think Mom had a lot of happy times because of the naughty thing I had done.

Chapter 35

Six Years Old

I WILL ALWAYS remember the day I turned six years old. My little brother's birthday was the day before mine. He had a party with everyone dressing up like cowboys and Indians, or wearing coonskin caps with a raccoon tail hanging down the back. The little cowboys boys wore holsters with toy guns and cowboy hats. The little Indians wore a band around their head with a feather in the back. They ate cake and ice-cream and had a good time. I was a girl and three years older, and I was not invited!

For my birthday, I was having a three-tiered cake. It was white on top, pink in the middle, and chocolate on bottom. Of course the bottom had to be chocolate because that was my favorite, and there had to be a lot of it.

My girlfriends from the neighborhood all came. I didn't know some of them very well because they lived too far away for me to play at their houses very often. One of them lived down a winding trail to the beach. The trail began at the dirt road that went from Carlson's Store and west to where it turned south. At the west end was where the trail began to my friend's house. Her older brother was a good friend of my brother Warren. My other friend that I didn't know very well lived near Aunt Virginia and Uncle Stanley. That was really far so I wouldn't be able to walk there for a couple more years!

My little brother Davey (we called him Davey because he like to pretend he was Davey Crocket) had been told he could not come to my party. My friends and I were going to play dress up. Mom had bought a bunch of long, pretty dresses at the rummage sale and lots of jewelry. She had also gotten quite a few hats, gloves, purses, etc. My friends were also bringing what they had to share.

We had the best time putting on the dresses, parading around to model for each other, and then changing into another ensemble. It was great fun until my little brother intruded!

He wanted to dress up too! He cried and carried on until Mom said we had to let him play with us. Oh brother! (No pun intended.) He always got his way by crying. When we sat down at the big dining room table, he had to sit with us and eat cake and ice-cream too. We had a good time, but I was annoyed that he had crashed my party. I had been good and stayed away from his and he had ruined mine! (That happened for the next three years!)

After cake and ice-cream, it was time to open presents. I can't remember any of the gifts I received from my girlfriends. I'm sure I loved every one of them. The gift I remember and cherished for many years was from my mom. It was a doll with green hair. She had a bottle that I could fill with water and she would drink it. She had a hole in her bottom and she would wet her diaper after she drank her bottle! I loved her instantly. I named her Sweet Sue. I now had Suzabella and Sweet Sue. Susy or any version of Susan was my favorite girl's name. I had another doll name Susie-Q, but she didn't last long. Suzabella and Sweet Sue were well-made dolls that could last a lifetime. (They would have, if I hadn't let my future little sister play with them.)

I was six years old. My girlfriends were as excited as me because some of us would be going to school for the first time. We would be in the first grade at the new Captain Charles Wilkes School.

After my party, Mom drove some of us to see the new school. It was mostly brick and windows. There was a huge playground. We met a nice man who said he was the Principal. He showed us where the 1st and 2nd grade classrooms were. I was really excited. I would ride the school bus and be gone all day just like my older brothers. Best of all, I would be away from my little brother; he really did annoy me!

CHAPTER 36

First Grade

SEPTEMBER CAME AND the long anticipated first day of school. I had a new dress and a lunch box. It had been a hard decision to choose a lunch box. There were so many to choose from. I got a pink one because pink and blue were my favorite colors. I carried all sorts of items in my lunch box, not just food. I had pencils, crayons, erasers, scissors, paste, and whatever else I needed to carry that would fit inside. Almost every day I carried the lunch box, I had something extra inside. However, most of the time I bought hot lunch.

The lady that cooked the lunches and served them was a good friend of my mother's. She told Mom that it was cheaper for her to pay for hot lunch than to make our lunch at home. Mom never really believed that, but she wanted her friend to think we could afford to buy the hot lunch.

The hot lunch was delivered to our hallway via a large metal cart that had a bunch of openings to hold the big pots and pans the food was in. I don't know how the lunch lady could push that huge cart. She was not a big lady and that cart was so big, it could barely fit through the wide doorway into our hall. It was at least twice as long as it was wide. We would line up at the door to our room, and in a single file, march out to the lunch cart, pick up a tray, our silverware and napkin, and hold it while the lunch lady put the food into the different sections on the tray. We said thank you as we grabbed a little carton of milk and headed back to our classroom to eat our lunch. When we were finished, we scraped the food remains from our tray into the garbage can at the back of the room, rinsed the tray in the sink, and stacked them for the lunch lady to pick up later.

My teacher's name was Miss Horlock. That was a strange name and she admitted it! She was so nice and taught us so many things. We learned the alphabet. The letters were pinned onto the wall around the perimeter of our room, up above the blackboard, doorway, and windows. Our numbers were on the walls in various places and also lots of interesting pictures. Our teacher knew a lot of stuff and wanted us to know it too! Just like in Sunday school, she taught us songs with actions, and we learned lessons through singing. We all knew Twinkle Little Star and she taught us the ABC Song to the same tune. There were so many songs for numbers and counting. We learned to raise our hand and wait to be called on before we could ask a question. We learned to not talk to our friends when the teacher was talking. We learned to use the restroom during recess and lunch.

One time my friend raised his hand and asked if he could go to the restroom. Miss Horlock said that recess was in five minutes and he could wait. Wrong! He couldn't wait, and he made a great big puddle underneath his chair and desk! I looked over at the floor in the row beside me and watched a puddle spread out around him. I glanced up at him, and saw that his face was very red, with tears streaming down his cheeks. I didn't like Miss Horlock very much right then. She saw the problem from the front of the classroom, and told my friend to stay there when the rest of us were excused to go out to recess. When we came back in, the puddle was cleaned up, and my friend had gone home for the day.

I quickly got over my dislike of Miss Horlock and decided that she was the best teacher ever. I invited her to dinner at our house which she happily accepted. That began a tradition in our home that lasted through the fifth grade!

School bus rides, playground activities, and classrooms gave a gregarious little girl like me opportunities for making new friends and becoming closer to the ones I already had. I learned about Valentine's Day. We made Valentine's at school to put in our Valentine holders that were taped to our desks. We made Valentine's for our moms and dads. We sang the same songs for Christmas that we sang in Sunday school. (Back then the real meaning of Christmas was celebrated and no one was offended by it. We would have been shocked if someone had objected!) We also sang fun songs about Santa Clause, but we knew that Jesus was the "reason for the season."

Everyone looked forward to the end of the year and the annual school picnic. Each class had their own picnic; it was a time for the students and teacher to say goodbye and have a special bonding that could not take place in the classroom setting. I was lucky because I had great bonding time when my teachers came to my house for dinner. There were two really wonderful things about my first year in school. I got a new best friend and the little sister I always wanted!

CHAPTER 37

Best Friend

WITH SCHOOL CAME a new best friend. We knew each other well and had played together often. However, school gave us the opportunity to see and play with each other every day. Her bus stop in the morning was a few stops before mine. She always saved me a seat, so I could sit with her when I got on. Going home, I got off before her. Sometimes she had a note from her mother to let her get off with me and sometimes I had a note from my mom saying to let me stay on the bus and get off with her. We played together after school during the autumn and in the spring when the days grew longer.

We were in the same classroom at school which made going to school all the more fun. We would play together during recess with a lot of the other girls; we all loved to jump rope. My best friend taught me how to play hop scotch. She knew how to play really well because she had gotten a hop scotch at her house. When I started going to her house after school, we played hop scotch almost every time I was there.

I like to play at her house more than I liked to have her come to mine. My little brother Davey always wanted to intrude on whatever we were doing. I think it annoyed her just as much as it annoyed me! She had an older brother, but he never bothered us and we stayed away from him. She had hop scotch and a teeter-totter that we had to put together when we wanted to play on it. It consisted of a saw horse that had an indent cut out of the top, just wide enough for the big board that we put across the saw horse. My friend was a little taller and heavier than me, so we put a little more board on my side. I don't know how we figured out why or how that would work, but we did. Of course, we were girls and girls were smart!

My friend's grandparents lived on the other side of her. We could take a trail to their house. We would go there and get eggs when her mom needed them (her grandpa was the chicken farmer). We could also walk from her grandparent's house to the post office and pick up their mail and her parent's mail. I could pick up ours too (if there was any for us). (The post office closed for business shortly thereafter, and we all got mail boxes that sat on posts, sometimes in long rows, on the side of the street. All along our narrow little street, there were mail boxes on the east side of the road. That was because the mailman drove down our street from the south end to the north end and had all the stops on the right side of the street.)

My friend and I started sleeping over at each other's house. That was really fun. We would talk and giggle most of the night. My friend had chores to do in the morning and I would help her. If we stayed up too late, we still had to get up in time to do the chores. Her mom would tell us, "There's no rest for the wicked and the righteous don't need any." We would just laugh; we had no idea what that meant.

My friend's mom made the best chocolate cake in the whole, wide world! She called it Buttermilk Chocolate Cake and it was my favorite. It was moist and rich, absolutely perfect! It was also covered with rich, dark, chocolate frosting. Whenever I went over there to play, whether it was after school or on the weekend, there was always Buttermilk Chocolate Cake waiting for me. My friend liked it too, but not as much as I did. Her mom thought it was so funny; I could hear her talking to my mom on the phone about it. I also heard her telling my mom that I could stay as long as Mom needed me to.

CHAPTER 38

Baby Sister

MY FRIEND'S MOM said we needed to go to my house and get some of my things so I could spend the night. We got really happy and excited about that; we loved spending the night together and this time it was spur of the momen, not even planned! We quickly walked to my house to get my pajamas and some other things and put them into my little red suitcase. Mom was sitting at the dining table looking like she wasn't feeling very good. My dad was telling my little brother to be good and listen to his aunt. Aunt Jessie was at our house. My cousins, Neal and Carol, were at their home with my Uncle Allen. Mom said she was going to the doctor to have a baby!

I had known for some time that we were going to have a new addition to the family; my mom was getting fatter and I had asked why. I just kept hoping the baby would be a girl and not a boy. I already had three brothers and there were five boys in the Tribe next door. I think I deserved a sister. (I hadn't thought about it at the time, but I'm sure my mother thought she deserved a daughter.)

I gave my mom and dad a hug and a kiss and my friend and I hurried back to her house. I could hardly wait to tell my friend's mom the news. When we went inside, the first thing she asked was, "Do you have some news?" I knew by the look on her face that she already knew my news. I just laughed and said mom was going to the doctor to have a baby. (I wondered how long it would take till I got a phone call.)

My friend's mom did not try and make us go to sleep that night. She seemed just as anxious as I was. She made a big bowl of popped corn and made popcorn balls out of some and the rest we ate with melted butter and salt. We listened to records, played games, and my friend's mom read us stories. We got really tired and just couldn't stay awake any longer. We went to bed, wanting to know if I had a new brother or sister, but no phone call came.

The next morning we got up and did the chores. Then we sat down to a breakfast of pancakes, eggs, and bacon. I really wasn't very hungry; I just wanted the phone to ring. Just as breakfast was over, the phone rang. My heart began to pound in my chest; my throat got really tight and dry. My friend's mom answered the phone and said, "Hello; it's for you," as she handed me the receiver. I put the black receiver to my ear and timidly said, "Hello."

My mom's voice was on the other end. She gave me the magic words I had been wishing for, "You have a baby sister!"

I was so happy; I began screaming with delight and jumping up and down. My friend knew instantly what the good news was and she started screaming and jumping up and down with me. Her mom was laughing and took the receiver out of my hand. She talked with my mom for a few more minutes and then hung up. She said I could stay all day. We didn't go to school that day; we hadn't had enough sleep and my friend's mom knew we wouldn't learn anything that day!

I went home that evening. My new little sister was laying in a white bassinette in the living room. She looked just like a baby doll. Her name was Susy!

CHAPTER 39

Chicken Pox

CHILDHOOD DISEASES WERE common when I was a little girl. Measles, Mumps, and Chicken Pox were always spreading from child to child, family to family. We were no exception. In fact, Mom tried to make us catch the illness when one of our friends had it. She said it was better to have it while we were young.

My best friend, whose home I stayed at when my little sister was born, caught the Mumps. Her brother had them too. Mom called her mom to see if I could go over there so I could catch them. I really didn't know what the Mumps were until I saw my friend. Her face was really fat, one side much more than the other! She was wearing a rolled up towel around her face; she said it was to keep her Mumps warm. I sat on her bed, and we talked and played Old Maid on her covers. She didn't really act like she was sick; she just looked funny.

After I had been there for a couple of hours her mom told me I needed to go home; she said I was probably there long enough to catch the Mumps. I never did catch them!

Every one of my friends had the measles, but I never caught them. The doctor told my mother that I must have a natural immunity to them, or else I had them as a baby and she never knew it. He said it was surprising that I didn't catch them because I had so many problems. (I didn't know what he was talking about.)

One morning, when I awoke to get up for school, I felt itchy all over. I looked at myself and was surprised because I was covered in red bumps. My brother Warren was covered in them too! Mom called the doctor and he came to our house. Sure enough, we both had the Chicken Pox.

We had two sofas in our living room and mom put us both to bed on the sofas. We were one of the first people in the neighborhood to have a television set, so we laid on the sofas and watched TV while we scratched our red bumps. Mom kept telling us not to scratch because it would leave a scar. She also said we would go blind watching TV while we had the Chicken Pox, but we made such a fuss, she took a chance and let us watch. We watched shows like, "Queen for a Day," and "Wunda, Wunda."

It was really hard not to scratch. Mom tried letting us soak in the bathtub with baking soda in the water. I think it made the itch worse. My brother got to soak first; he used too much hot water, so I got a very shallow tub of water. Sitting on top of the register felt good, but mom said we would itch more. (Sometimes, I thought Mom would tell us something awful would happen to us, just to make us not do whatever we wanted to do, that she didn't want us to do. Mom was always telling me I would get Polio if I played in the mud puddles or the water in the ditch on the side of the road. I played in the water all the time and I did not get Polio.)

My brother and I had those itchy bumps for a week. I had bumps on the bottom of my feet and under my arms. I had one on my forehead that drove me nuts. I couldn't help scratching I, t and it broke and left a scab. When the scab healed, it left a scar. (To this day, I still have the scar.) Those Chicken Pox were the beginning of a lot of troublesome times for me!

CHAPTER 40

The Earache

I HAD SUFFERED earaches from the time I could remember. They didn't favor one ear or the other. Sometimes both ears ached at the same time. I was always going to see the doctor or he was always coming to see me. (In those days, doctors made house calls, especially when someone was really sick.) I had a fever and a very bad earache in my left ear. The doctor came late in the day, just as it was getting dark.

He looked into my ears and gave a little grunt. He gave my mom a bottle of drops and told her to put the drops in both my ears, three times a day. I was used to having water in my ears from swimming and from playing in the bathtub, but I hated having drops put into my ears. They especially hurt in my left ear. I cried and thought it was torture to have mom putting those nasty drops in my ears. Still, I tried to be brave and endure it.

As usual, when I was sick, I got to sleep on the sofa in the living room. I guessed it was easier for mom to take care of us if we were down stairs. Mom got me a hot water bottle and wrapped it in a towel because it was too hot to touch. She said, as the water cooled, I could unwrap it, so I could continue to feel the warmth on my ear. I fell asleep on the nice, warm, hot water bottle.

The next morning my ear wasn't hurting; it was plugged and sounded like my head was under the water. I sat up on the sofa and looked down at the crumpled towel laying over the hot water bottle. The towel had a bunch of yellow waxy substance on it. I felt it on my face and neck and could even see some on my pajama top. Yuck! My ear had leaked all over! I went to find Mom and show her the nasty mess that had dripped out of my ear. There was so much; it looked like it had poured out of my ear! My mother called the doctor and he said not to worry, just to keep using the drops until they were gone. (My mother never used medications until they were gone. If it was something that would keep for any length of time, she would save it in case we needed it again.)

That earache was the worst I had ever had. It seemed, from that point on, that my ear aches became more frequent and because of them I missed a lot of school. I had a sore throat often and the doctor called it Tonsillitis. I continued to get pneumonia in the spring and the fall. I missed a lot of school!

CHAPTER 41

The Christmas Pageant

THE CHRISTMAS THAT my sister was a new baby was really very special. Even though she was a girl, she was going to be Baby Jesus in a Christmas pageant at the Seabold Community Church. I was so excited because she was my baby sister, so I thought it meant that I would be Mary. WRONG!

The parts in the pageant were assigned and I was one of the angels. My friend, where our dog Boots was staying, was chosen to be Mary. She was very pretty dressed as Mary. The angels looked good too. We wore white gowns and had golden, shimmering garlands in our hair for halos. Most of the boys wore bathrobes and towels on their heads with a band tied around their forehead to hold the towel in place. The boys that played the Wise Men got to wear fancy robes. They carried jewelry boxes as gifts for Baby Jesus.

Our Sunday school practiced the pageant when the grownups were in Sunday school class on Sundays and as time drew near the date of the pageant, we practiced on Saturdays too. Just before the big show, a decision was made to use a doll instead of my little sister. Secretly I was glad a doll was used because I didn't think it was fair to not be Mary if my baby sister was Baby Jesus. (I had so much to learn about love, sharing, and life.)

The Christmas Pageant was held in the evening. There were lights on the sides of the chapel walls, between the windows. They glowed like candle light. I never knew if they were real candles or lights. However, the effect was the same. They made a soft, golden glow over the whole room. The Tribe's dad read the story of Jesus's birth from the Bible. As he read each part, we the actors, would march up to the stage and take our places to make the scene he was describing.

The stage got pretty crowded by the time we were through! Every one of the children in the Sunday school was up on the stage by the ending scene. Then we sang Silent Night and our parents joined in for the second and third verses.

When the pageant was over, we left the stage and found our parents sitting in the audience. I had been so jealous of my friend who played Mary. Now my heart was overflowing with Peace on Earth, Good Will toward Men. Obviously it was toward women too because all I felt was love!

CHAPTER 42

Valentine Be Mine

ONE OF THE most memorable events of the first grade was making Valentines. I had never heard of Valentine's Day before, and all of a sudden it became a very important day. Preparations began the first of February. February was such a short month, and we celebrated the birthdays of Presidents Lincoln and Washington, plus the wonderful day called Valentine's Day. Because there were three special days in the short month, our classroom was in a flurry of activity the entire month! When we weren't making decorations and hanging them up, we were taking them down to get ready to put up more. It seemed we had very little time for school work; participating in the classroom activities was how we learned.

Out teacher read us a story about St. Valentine. It was a sad story, but he was a very good man who helped many people. She told us that he performed many weddings and he was killed on February 14th hundreds of years ago. She said that's why on Valentine's Day you let people know how much you love them.

We were given big sheets of red paper. Our teacher showed us how to fold the paper in half and draw part of the letter C on the paper. Then we cut along the line we had drawn and when we opened the paper, it made a heart! This was really fun, like making paper dolls, only a lot easier. We had learned to cut out snowflakes earlier in the year and our teacher left them up on the walls. She said they were pretty with the red hearts. She was right!

Our teacher gave us white, paper doilies to put behind the red hearts. They looked just like the fancy Valentines in the store, well, almost. We got to write our names on the big hearts and helped to hang them around the room.

The next Valentine project was to make folders to tape to the front of our desks. We cut out two hearts the same size. Next we stood in line to use the stapler on the teacher's desk. We each stapled our hearts together around the edges, being sure to leave a wide opening at the top. We got to write our names on our hearts. After taping our hearts to the front of our desks, we had to clean up our mess. We spent a lot of time cleaning up our messes. I know if we had to do that much work at home, we wouldn't have liked it. However, here at school, it was great fun.

One day we made Valentine's for our parents. We used the same kind of red paper and white doilies. We used paste, glitter, crayons, or whatever we wanted to make our Valentines special for our parents. That was a very fun and messy project! I discovered that paste tasted like chewing gum; yum! Soon all the children were licking their fingers. Our teacher told us not to taste it; we would get tummy aches. (I don't remember any of us getting a stomach ache.)

We were told we could make Valentines at home to bring to school to put in the envelopes for the other children. We were given a list of names of everyone in the class so we could spell their names correctly. We could buy ready-made Valentines at the store or make them ourselves. I made Valentines that first year; I like to make things, just like my mom.

On Valentine's Day we had a party. A few of the mothers brought cookies, cupcakes and Kool-Aid. We ate our sweets and opened the Valentines that were stuffed into our hearts. We each had a Valentine from everyone in our class. I loved Valentine's Day!

CHAPTER 43

Escape from Little Brother

EASTER CAME THAT year on April 1st. It was not a warm, sunny day; it was a day for playing inside. After church, we all went to Grandma's house for the big, family dinner. As usual, all the kids sat at the kitchen table to eat, while the grownups ate in the dining room and at card tables set up in the living room. My little brother was really a pest by then.

After dinner, my cousin Neal, and my other cousin Nancy who lived in Seattle, and I went upstairs to one of the bedrooms where there were lots of books and board games. We shut the door so my little brother couldn't come in. We got out the Pickup Sticks and began playing in earnest. (It took a lot of concentration and a steady hand to win at Pickup Sticks.) My little brother figured out where we were and started crying outside the door.

We did our best to ignore him, but he was starting to cry really loud! Pretty soon I heard my dad outside the door asking him what all the fuss was about. David said something (he was very difficult to understand because he needed a speech therapist), and my dad opened the door and told us we had to let him play. A three or four year-old cannot play Pickup Sticks! They can't play Chinese checkers, or even American checkers! What could we do? There wasn't anything that my little brother could play with us that wouldn't ruin the game.

My cousin Nancy came up the plan for one of us to play with my little brother while two of us played a real game together. Then whoever won the real game, would play the next game with whoever was playing with my little brother. She was so smart because she was older and wiser! We took turns playing against each other and with my little brother. It wasn't as much fun, but at least he was quiet.

For the next few years we had to endure having my little brother find us and intrude on our game. We would sneak upstairs to the bedroom with all the games, and quietly close the door and be as quiet as mice so he wouldn't know we were there. We could usually play several rounds of Pickup Sticks, or a few games of checkers, before he would come crying at the door. Our cousin Nancy quit playing games with us after a few years, just about the time that we accepted my little brother David as old enough to join us.

CHAPTER 44

My Favorite Tree

I'M NOT SURE when I realized I loved to climb trees, the taller, the better. I knew my mother was terrified of high places, and that she got upset when I climbed higher than she thought was safe. I really wasn't sure what she thought was safe. I would climb the Plum trees and Apple trees when I wanted to eat fresh fruit or when Mom wanted to cook something that called for fruit that was growing outside in our back yard. So, it seemed perfectly reasonable to me, that if I felt safe in a tall tree, it was okay to climb it.

We had an unusually tall tree down near the end of our property. It grew just in front of the property that belonged to the people who lived down the zigzag beach trail. It was a Cedar tree and had branches that came all the way to the ground. It was a perfect tree for climbing. I could step onto the lowest branch and hold onto a higher one, as though I was walking up a ramp and holding onto a railing. The branches going up the tree seemed to be perfectly spaced, so that there was always a branch to grab when I needed one. The prickly boughs did not bother me because I climbed next to the big trunk and the branches were bare where I was climbing.

At first, I climbed only a short distance because I had never climbed so high before. Nevertheless, as the days went by, I found myself higher up in the tree where the wind could sway the tree top. This was great fun; why had I been so timid before? Every day, when I had the opportunity, I would climb that tree as high as I could go. I could see the Tribe's house when I looked toward the south. I could see the Olympic Mountains when I looked to the west. I could even see the Agate Pass Bridge and the cars going across it when I looked toward the north. When I looked toward the east, I could see our big porch that ran the entire length of our house. It looked like I was at eye level to the porch.

I thought that was really neat until my mother came out onto the porch and saw me!

"Oh My God!" she screamed with the most shrilling scream I had ever heard. She immediately began running back and forth the length of the porch, looking like she was pulling her hair. I had never seen my mother so upset! I started laughing so hard; it was the most hilarious thing I had ever seen. She was really beside herself. She kept screaming and I kept on laughing. My dad was fishing in Alaska, so she couldn't get any help from him.

"You get down from there right now!"

Why was she being so unreasonable? I was perfectly fine; I was safe up in the big tree and I knew it! With a big sigh, I began the tedious climb down; climbing down was much more difficult than climbing up. However, I was quite accomplished at both directions, so I made it down with no harm or accident. I slowly walked back up to the house, knowing I was in trouble again.

Mom informed me that I was not allowed to climb that tree ever again. I protested saying that my older brothers climbed the tree and so did the Tribe boys. I must have said the wrong thing because the Tribe's dad came over soon afterward and cut off the bottom branch.

Low branch or no branch, it didn't matter. That was my favorite tree and I continued to climb it. I had friends over to play and they climbed it to. We would see who could climb the highest and sway in the wind; it was so much fun. Mom gave up and realized kids will be kids.

Chapter 45

Bat in the Bedroom

My MOTHER HATED birds; she hated anything that could fly. I don't know what had happened to her that made her like she was; it seemed ridiculous to me. I loved birds and loved to pretend I could fly. I would even dream that I could fly. I was sure that people were meant to be able to fly because all my friends dreamed they could fly too.

My parents had been using the downstairs bedroom as theirs and decided to paint and wallpaper the big room upstairs for themselves. They painted the walls brown, which I thought was really dark and ugly! Next, they began putting wallpaper onto the upper halves of the walls. It looked like Hawaii looked in books. There were green palm leaves, brown coconuts, blue water and pretty Hawaiian girls with long, black hair and grass skirts.

It was a warm, summer evening and dad was home from Alaska. I was up in their room watching the wall papering process. It looked like a lot of work, but they kept at it, determined to get the job done that night. My brothers were downstairs watching television. (We were very fortunate to have a television; they were not a common commodity.) The smells in the room were bothering me and mom said to open the window. (I should have left the room but we didn't think about the effect of fumes on my fragile lungs or on any other part of me.)

With the window open, and the fresh air blowing in, the room was much more pleasant and I settled down to watch the work progress. Mom and Dad were both over by the double doorway. Mom was using a roller to put glue on the wall. Dad was putting the paper over the gluey wall and pressing it down with his big hands. They seemed to be having fun because they were laughing.

All of a sudden a bat flew in through the open window! I had seen bats outside in the evenings, and I thought they were birds that flew at nighttime. I had never seen a bat in our house before. The light was on, and it was fun to watch the bat flying round the room, acting like it wanted to find its way back out into the night. It flew around several times and mom started screaming, "Oh My God!"

She dropped the roller and tried to escape out the open double doors. Of all the people in the whole world, this could only happen to my mom. The bat flew into her hair! She let out the most blood curdling scream. It was even louder and more frantic than when I was up in the tree! She was beside herself; she didn't know what to do. She wanted to reach up and pull it out, but she was afraid of being bit.

My dad grabbed the broom that was leaning against the wall and began beating on my mom's head, trying to get the bat to fly away. Mom was bending over and covering her head with her arms, while my dad was beating her head with the broom. It was positively the funniest thing I had seen yet! The poor bat finally succumbed to the beating broom and dropped to the floor in a small, furry heap. I looked at that little animal, laying there so limp and still. It wasn't a bird at all, just a cute little mouse like animal that happed to be able to fly.

My mother sat down on the floor and had a good cry while my dad scooped up the bat into the dust pan and went downstairs. When he came back, they cleaned up the mess and decided to finish the next day when there were no bats to fly inside and disturb their work.

CHAPTER 46

Second Grade

My 7th BIRTHDAY came and went with nothing happening out of the ordinary. My little brother David crashed my party and I was upset with him, nothing new. My oldest brother Jerry thought up a wonderful game for the younger kids in the neighborhood, "Glue Man."

He would lie on the grass in the back yard, and all of us little kids would try and run close by him without getting caught. If he managed to catch one of us by the arm or leg, the rest of us would try and free the caught kid. We had loads of fun and so did my big brother.

All sorts of fruit was ripening in the trees and the blackberries were getting ripe too. There was plenty of picking, gathering, and preserving going on at our house. In the midst of all the commotion, it was time to head back to school.

Mom had made me some new dresses and bought me some other things at the Seabold Rummage Sale. We also went to some other rummage sales, but I don't remember where they were. Mom took me to the Winslow Department Store to get new saddle shoes. The doctor told my mother to never put someone else's shoes on my feet. I was glad because I liked to get new shoes. The problem was I had narrow feet. It was hard to find shoes that my feet didn't slide around in. In addition to that, my ankle bones were below the top of the shoe openings and my ankles would get the skin rubbed off. I had to wear lifts inside my shoes; they didn't help much.

The first day of second grade, I was so excited. My friend down the street, who got on the bus several stops before me, had promised to save me a seat on the bus. I walked with my brother Warren and some of the boys from the Tribe next door. We walked to the bus stop at the Carlson's store. There were other friends there too. One of my good friends was just starting first grade that day. I didn't care that she was only in the first grade, she was still my friend.

When the bus came, we quickly lined up and got on the bus in a very orderly fashion. Some of the parents were there which is probably why we were so well behaved. I quickly looked for my friend I was going to sit with, and she was sitting with some other girls. The boys were on one side and the girls on the other side. There were no seats being saved; we had to fill up from the back to the front! (Fortunately for us, that seating arrangement didn't last long. We had a new bus driver and it was easier for him to learn what child belonged at what stop when we sat in the order we got on the bus.)

As soon as we got to school, we met up with our friends and went to find our new classroom and teacher. She had our names on a sheet of paper and checked us off as we went through the door. She said our names were on a colored strip of paper attached to the front of our desks. We just had to find our name and we would know where we were supposed to sit. We had to hang our sweaters or jackets in the coat closet and if it was raining, we put our boots in there too. I was way in the back of the room, not in the very back, but close to it on the side near the windows. My best friend was way up in the opposite corner!

Second grade was a lot harder than first grade! We were the group that didn't have Kindergarten and we were not expected to know much when we went to First grade. However, we were now in the Second grade and we were expected to know our A, B, Cs and how to write them. We could write simple words and sentences. We could read simple books. We knew how to behave properly in the classroom and on the playground. We already knew so much, it didn't seem like there was anything else we needed to learn. WRONG!

We learned how to write letters to other children in another state; they were called pen pals. We wrote to them; they wrote to us. We learned how to add and subtract two digit numbers. We learned to read books that had real words and names of real children instead of Dick and Jane, Sally, and Bobby. I did know several Jane's and I knew a couple Bobby's but I didn't know any Sally's and I remember one Dick that was a friend of my older brother's. I liked reading in the Second grade much better than in the First.

I can't remember having to get shots and vaccinations in the First grade. Perhaps we did and I just can't remember. I have a vague memory of going to the old Bainbridge Review Building and getting some sort of shot in order to go to First grade. (It was so long ago; it's a dim memory.) But I can remember the shots in the Second grade! We had to line up out in the hallway with our sleeve rolled up. Each of us, in turn, had to get a Polio Shot or a Small Pox vaccination. The shots just made our arms red and swollen, but the vaccination made a bump that turned into a blister, then a scab, and finally would peel off and leave a scar. Everyone always compared their vaccination scars.

After a few weeks of school, I started not feeling well. I was still plagued with earaches and sore throats. I had joined the Blue Birds and was having fun with that group of girls once a week after school. Unfortunately, I didn't even feel like going to Blue Birds. I was tired all the time; Mom told the doctor that I was lethargic. The doctor decided that I needed allergy tests. That meant missing even more school. I was having so many problems that Mom and my teacher decided it would be best for me to stay home and do my school work at home. Once in a while, I could go to school if I was feeling up to it.

CHAPTER 47

Allergy Tests

My mother and I had to go to Seattle to the Children's Orthopedic Hospital for me to get the allergy tests. I had some preliminary tests at the clinic in Winslow, but I had a bad reaction to every spot the nurse had put the drops on and broken my skin. The doctor said I needed extensive testing. I wasn't attending school, so I didn't need to worry about missing class. However, I didn't want to go back to that hospital; I hated it!

The first time we went, I had an ominous feeling that something would go wrong; I was right. It began when we went to buy our tickets at the desk behind the window in the big ferry terminal building. I could read and the sign said for children 6 years and older the cost was 50 cents. Mom paid for herself and said I was under age! I tried to correct her and remind her that I was seven years old. She grabbed me by the arm and shushed me as she quickly pulled me away from the ticket booth. She told me I was small like a 5 year old and to not let anyone know any different!

We rode the ferry boat to the other side, and when we got off, we walked up to the next street to catch a bus. That was a new experience for me; usually we took a taxi because I was sick. I was feeling OK that day, so Mom said we would take the bus. We were waiting for the people on the bus to get off before we got on. To my surprise, a little lady got off the bus. She was only a little bigger than me! I yelled and pointed to the lady saying, "Look Mom, a midget!"

Mom grabbed my arm and pulled me close to her and shook her finger in my face while scolding me. "Don't you ever say that in front of somebody again! If you see a midget or a person with one arm or leg, or whatever, you just keep your mouth shut!"

I felt terrible. The little lady smiled at me and I could tell she wasn't mad at me. But my Mom was really out of sorts that day. (Looking back, I'm sure she was nervous wondering what my test results would show.) We got on the bus and took the long ride to the hospital. I recognized the big waiting room immediately; some things never change. At least no one came with a wheel chair or a crib to get me that day!

Mom checked with the lady at the reception desk and then we waited for a Candy Striper to come and escort us to the room where the allergy tests were given. She came all too soon! I had a bad feeling about what was going to happen to me; I hated the hospital! When we got to the room, I was told to take off everything but my panties and to put the blue gown on. Then I was supposed to lay on the bed facing down. I could put my face between two pillows to breath; that really didn't work very well. I had tests just like at the clinic, only a whole lot more. The nurse made little x's in rows down my back and down my legs. She then put a drop of liquid on each drop and made a mark on a chart. Then she broke my skin where each drop was. She used something that looked like the little screwdriver to my mom's sewing machine.

Mom and I waited what seemed like a very long time. I was cold and I couldn't put a blanket on. I could hear the child in the bed behind the curtain saying he was cold too. Pretty soon, a Candy Striper came in with a heater to warm us up; that helped quite a bit. After a while, a doctor came in a looked at all my spots. He said to get dressed and comeback in a couple more days. So home we went. I had an ice-cream cone on the ferry which helped me feel better. I was not happy; I needed to go back in a couple days.

The next day I was supposed to do school work, but I didn't want to. The work books were hard for me to understand what I was supposed to do. Mom was no help; she didn't understand either. I tried to ask my best friend, but she wasn't much help; she just wanted to play. I wanted to play and also eat her mom's chocolate cake. I could not seem to get enough of it!

The next day Mom and I went back to the hospital. I was good at the Ferry terminal and didn't say anything about being seven years old. We took the bus again, but I didn't get to see the little lady ever again. At the hospital, after checking in, we went right to the room without an escort.

The doctor looked at all my spots, made some notes on his chart, and then had me lay on my back. The nurse did just what she had done the other day. She x'd me with a pen, put drops of liquid on the x's and then broke my skin under each drop. I stayed there a long time and the doctor came in and had a look as he wrote things on the chart. Then the bad news! He said I had to come back next week and do it again! By the time I was done with all my allergy tests, we made six trips to the hospital. My mom was given a whole list of things I was allergic to and it was awful!

I was allergic to chocolate! My favorite food in the whole world and that terrible doctor told my mother I couldn't eat it anymore! I also couldn't eat peanut butter, salmon, and a bunch of vegetables. (I didn't mind that very much.) I was also allergic to dust, all types of pollen, chicken feathers, horses, cats, dogs, and chenille. The first thing my mother did was to call my friend's mom and inform her I was not to have any chocolate cake when I went there to play. I knew I had a bad feeling about going to that hospital!

I tried to go to my friend's house often. Her mom sneaked me the chocolate cake because I said it never made me sick. It was the truth; I never felt sick from eating chocolate cake or anything else that was chocolate. I never felt sick from eating anything that was on the list the doctor gave my mother. I did get asthma from dust and pollen, and from cats and dogs, and from horses too.

My mother and I had to return to the hospital a few more times so I could get shots of something that was supposed to make me not allergic anymore. I don't know if it worked or not. I just learned to avoid the things that gave me asthma.

CHAPTER 48

Blue Birds

IN THE SECOND grade, it was very common for little girls to either join the Blue Birds or the Brownies. All the little girls in my neighborhood were becoming Blue Birds because one of the mother's said she would be the leader. We all knew each other, so it seemed perfectly logical for us to get together on a weekday after school. We got to wear our Blue Bird uniforms to school on that day, which made us feel very important.

I went to school the first few weeks. That made going to Blue Birds very easy because I would get off the bus with the other girls and we would go to my friend's house and have Blue Birds. Unfortunately, very early in the school year, I started having more health issues and with the allergy tests and constant trips to Seattle, it was difficult for me to attend Blue Birds on a regular basis. I loved going to my friend's house after school and doing fun activities with the other girls. When my mother brought me on those occasions when I could attend, I began to feel less and less welcomed.

At first everyone wanted to know why I wasn't at school and seemed genuinely concerned. There were always hugs and words of encouragement. I knew I was among friends. But, as the weeks went by, it became apparent that they had grown weary of my illness and were more interested in their friends they saw every day instead of the little, sick girl who showed up occasionally. There were no more welcoming hugs, no more kind words, in fact, they snubbed me!

I continued to attend on those occasions when the leader insisted and she promised that the other girls would be nice to me. I endured because I didn't want anyone to think I was a quitter. The house where we met was really old and worn. During that year, the leader had a new house being built. One day when Mom drove me to Blue Birds, the girls were meeting in the new house. We had to remove our shoes before we went inside. The floors and carpet were white; I had never been in a house with white carpet and floors! We all knew we had to do everything possible to not make a mess. We couldn't spill anything!

Our leader made sure we didn't mess up her new house. We had to go outside when we did any project that was messy in any way. We had to eat our refreshments outdoors too. These arrangements were fine on a warm, sunny afternoon. However, in Western Washington, those days are not so common as in other parts of the United States. (I knew that because I learned it by reading the Weekly News Reader we got at school. When I couldn't attend school, my neighbors brought them to me.) Sitting outside in the cold was not good for me. I got sick with another bout of pneumonia.

I quit going to Blue Birds and quit even trying to go to school. I didn't want to work on my homework and I ended up spending my days watching the television. I enjoyed watching television and learned all kinds of interesting things. I felt like watching television was much better than going to school! In the afternoon there was a show called, "Brakeman Bill." Lots of times there were Girl Scout Troops, Brownie Troops, Boy Scouts, Cub Scouts, Campfire Girls, and Blue Birds as visitors on the show. I was glad that my Blue Bird Troop was never on; that would have made me feel really horrible.

The end of the school year was fast approaching. The weather had warmed and I was feeling much better. The allergy shots must have been working because I wasn't having so many problems. I decided to go back to school. I was excited and really looking forward to it; maybe I could even go to Blue Birds again.

CHAPTER 49

Attacked

I WENT BACK to my Second grade class on a warm, spring day, late in the school year. My desk was still in its place near the back, close to the windows. Some of the kids who sat near me asked, "Who are you?"

I was surprised they couldn't remember me; I could remember them. I couldn't understand how they could not remember me. I hadn't been gone that long! I had come back to school several times during the year, so it seemed ridiculous to me that I could be so quickly forgotten. My teacher reintroduced me to class as though I were a new student. (That really embarrassed me!)

At the lunch recess, I played with my friends just like I used to. I had fun jumping rope, swinging, and playing hopscotch. When the bell rang, we all quit playing and ran towards the covered shelter between the First and Second Grade building and the Third and Fourth Grade building. The covered shelter was a huge area with a cement floor. The roof was really high and we could play outdoor games in the shelter during bad weather. It was also where we would line up after recess to return to our classrooms.

I was a lot smaller than my classmates and lagged behind when we ran to get in line. I had barely made it to the shelter when most of the kids had already entered the double doors into our building. There was a group of four boys from my classroom that lingered out in the shelter like they were waiting for me. They started walking toward me as I approached the double doors.

Two of the boys grabbed my arms, one on each side. They dragged me out near the edge of the sheltered play area. The other two boys grabbed my feet and pulled them out from under me. I screamed as my head banged the cement floor!

I screamed and cried and squirmed to escape their grasps. It was no use; I was far outnumbered and I was still in a weakened condition. I was also very small for my age and two of those boys were the biggest in our class.

They held me upside down and stared at my panties! They talked about my panties and about how they would be nice and keep them on me. Then one of the boys, (I remember the names of all these boys) took out a pocket knife! I screamed and wiggled some more, trying to escape and only making them grab me tighter. The boy with the knife managed to get it open and while the three other boys held me captive, upside down and screaming, he proceeded to cut my thumb! He sliced it right along my right thumbnail. It hurt badly! My head was throbbing, my heart was pounding, my voice was gone, and my thumb was throbbing right along with my beating heart!

All of a sudden, they dropped me in a heap on the cold, hard cement and ran back through the double doors. I laid there on the floor, silently sobbing because I had no voice and wishing I had not come back to school. I knew I needed to get up, but I was shaking so much and I felt so sick, it took every ounce of strength and fortitude I could muster to get up off that cold, hard floor. I walked to the double doors on wobbling legs, my teeth chattering as though it were mid-winter.

No teacher was standing at the double doors. Usually, at least one of the teachers waited at the doors until the last student was inside. (I guess because no one was used to me being there, they just forgot about me.) I was so weak and wobbly that I could not open the big door. I banged on the door with my fist until my First grade teacher came and opened the door for me. (My first grade room was the closest to the double doors.) Miss Horlock was very upset when she saw me and without waiting to be asked, I sobbed out my story of horror and pain. I could scarcely speak, my voice was so horse, but she understood and took me by the hand down the hallway to my Second grade classroom.

Miss Horlock came into the room with me and took me to my teacher's desk. She told my teacher what had happened to me. My teacher asked me to tell her what boys had done this cruel thing to me. I told her and she called them up to her desk. She used the phone on the wall behind her desk to call the school office. The janitor showed up at our classroom in a matter of seconds! He took those naughty boys with him and my teacher took me to the back of the room and washed my hands and face and put a bandage on my thumb.

I went back to my seat; I cannot remember learning anything the rest of that day. I just wanted to go home! After an hour, those boys came back to our classroom. The boys' faces were very red and they had been crying. One of the boys who sat across from me, and sat behind one of my attackers, asked him what happened. He said the janitor had blown smoke in their eyes. That sounded like an awful punishment and it quickly spread around the room. Those naughty boys were pitied by the rest of the class and I was the culprit who had brought that terrible punishment upon them!

No one felt the least bit sorry for me. No teacher tried to comfort me. I sat there, at my desk, the rest of the afternoon, enduring the pain in my thumb and my head, waiting to go home. When the bell finally rang, I gratefully picked up my things and walked out the door. I rode the bus home in silence that day and walked slowly back to my house after getting off at my stop. I didn't want to play with any of my friends; I just wanted to go home and have my mother hug me.

CHAPTER 50

School Picnic

MY SECOND GRADE teacher phoned my mother to let her know that I was going to be held back in the second grad for another year. She also told my mother about the school picnic to be held at the Fay Bainbridge State Park and that if I wanted to come, I was welcome. Mom said that I would love to come without even asking me. I protested, but Mom said we would just be playing, so I should go. She said that she would stay there with me the entire time; that made me feel a little better.

I had healed up from my ordeal at school, but I had not gone back. I knew that I was going to flunk, so it didn't matter to me that I missed more school. I was embarrassed and scared to go back; those kids were mean! My close friends were still nice to me, but they didn't really know what to say or do to make me feel better.

The day before the school picnic, I was over at the Tribe's house playing baseball in their field. I was standing near the second base, trying to catch a fly ball. The littlest Tribe brother was running from first to second base. Someone yelled at him to keep on running around to third. I was barefoot and he stepped on my little toe as he ran across the base. It broke the skin on my toe, but I wanted to keep playing. (When I played with the Tribe I was happy and always had fun.) I continued to play until the sun was low and we had to go inside. I walked home and took my bath to get ready for bed. I didn't even tell Mom that my toe had been hurt; it seemed so insignificant in relation to other things that had happened to me.

I was dreading the school picnic and went to bed wishing that I didn't need to go. I must have wished too hard, because when I woke up the next morning, my toe was red and swollen. There was a wide, red line going from the sore on my little toe, up the side of my leg, almost half way between my ankle and my knee. I knew that wasn't good! I ran down the stairs and into the kitchen to show my mother the strange red line on my leg.

"Oh My God!" My mother used her favorite phrase again.

She quickly was at the telephone, calling the doctor. I heard her side of the conversation, "Vicki has an infected toe and it looks like blood poisoning. There is a red streak going from her toe up the side of her leg!"

Mom hung up the phone and said we needed to go to the doctor as soon as we finished breakfast. My busy mother had to get my little brother and baby sister ready for the day, feed my sister, pack a bunch of stuff for both my brother and sister, plus get herself ready. My older brothers fended for themselves very well. (Looking back I realize now that my older brothers needed a lot more attention than they got.) I occupied a lot of my mother's precious time; today was no different.

We set off in the big Pontiac. I sat in the front seat that day; I was nervous about going to the doctor again. What was blood poisoning? I didn't feel sick, just scared! We had to drive all the way to Winslow. That long drive gave me more time to think about all the horrible things blood poisoning could be. I had to pretend to be brave and act like everything was fine.

When we got to the doctor's office, we didn't need to wait out in the waiting room; we went right into an exam room and I climbed up onto the table that was covered with white paper. The nurse had me take off my shoe and sock. She asked me if it hurt and I told her it didn't. (Like that was going to make everything better.) She went to get the doctor. He came in, wearing his white smock with his stethoscope hanging from his neck. He greeted me with his usual smile (a sure sign something was wrong) and took my foot in his big, warm hand. He had some kind of glasses that he used to look at the red line. He said my mom was correct, it was blood poisoning.

He said the cure was fast and easy. All I needed was a shot of penicillin! I had had those shots before; it was not easy. True, they may be fast, but they were not easy. Perhaps he used the word easy because it was easy for the nurse to give me a shot. However, getting a shot in the butt hurts. It hurts when you get the shot and it hurts much worse as time goes by. When I got a shot, it would swell and be red for several days. Often I would feel sicker from the shot than from whatever was ailing me. I tried to protest because I was going to the school picnic and said maybe I should get the shot after the picnic.

No one thought that was a good idea. They said the sooner I got the penicillin in me, the faster I would get better. I kept thinking I wasn't sick; I felt fine except for a sore toe. Needless to say, I got the shot and we went to the Fay Bainbridge State Park for my Second grade class picnic.

We arrived after everyone else was already there. The kids were playing on the swings and slide. They were climbing on the monkey bars. I didn't want to play; my butt was burning where I had gotten the shot. I sat at the picnic table where my mom was talking to my teacher. My teacher kept shaking her head, saying that was too bad I was such a sick little girl. Then she looked at me and said if I had been a good girl and done my homework, I could have passed Second grade and been going into the Third grade for the next school year. She made me feel worse!

Mom kept pestering me to go and swing or slide. I told her the shot hurt and I didn't want to. She insisted that playing would make it feel better. Where do grownups get those stupid ideas? How does sliding down a slide on your bottom help your bottom feel better when it's already sore? How can sitting on a hard swing, or worse, one of the swings that had a rubber strip that fit right to your bottom when you sat on it, make you feel better? Sometimes I felt like Mom wasn't as smart as she was at other times. This was one of those times I wished she would just let me be still, stay right where I was, and not move a muscle. Alas, I gave in to her pestering.

I walked up the hill to where all the play equipment was and chose to climb the ladder to the slide. Climbing wasn't too bad, but I had a terrible time trying to maneuver my body into the correct position to sit on the slide for the ride down. By then, the painful swelling had settled in, and my butt was on fire. I went down the slide only once and walked slowly back to the picnic table. I told my mom that I was sick. My teacher gave me my report card and said she hoped I would feel better. A few of the kids said good-bye to me, but most of them went right on playing, not even noticing that I had been there.

(I knew I had flunked, so I didn't bother to look at my report card. I opened it out of sheer curiosity when I was 12 years old. There was a lime flavored sucker taped to the inside of the card. I ate the sucker; it was very sweet and gooey. My report card was full of Insufficients!)

CHAPTER 51

The Vitamin Drink

AFTER A YEAR of illness and flunking the Second grade, I thought things couldn't get much worse. WRONG! I don't know why I was an eternal optimist when life kept teaching me lesson after lesson that if something could go wrong, it probably would. I slowly healed up from the penicillin shot (always worse than the doctor said it would be) and my toe got better. It was summer, the weather was warm, and I thought I would have a fun summer.

The doctor told my mother that he was sure my tonsils were poisoning my body and that he better take them out. However, because I was such a sickly child, I needed to take a vitamin drink to help build me up. He wanted to remove my tonsils before my 8th birthday so that I would have time to heal completely before going back to school. He promised both me and my mother that after I had my tonsils removed, I would feel like a brand new person. (He was smiling at me while he said it, so I had my doubts.)

Mom and I went to the Drug Store in Winslow and I got the brown bottle of vitamin mixture that the pharmacist mixed up especially for me. He said I was a lucky little girl because I was going to feel really good by the time I was finished with the bottle. He didn't warn me about the smell or the taste!

I was supposed to drink the vitamin mixture in a glass of juice or milk because that would help mask the flavor. WRONG! I could smell the horrid stuff the second my mother removed the cap from the bottle. Even she turned her head away in disgust and held her breath while she poured the capful into my orange juice. She actually admonished me to hold my breath while I drank the juice because then it wouldn't taste as bad. WRONG!

I immediately gagged when the liquid entered my mouth. I barely tasted it when I had to set the glass down and rush to the bathroom to throw up the nasty stuff plus everything else that was in my stomach! I started crying and I was shaking all over. My mother called the doctor and he said I had to drink it. He said that now that my stomach was empty, I wouldn't have anything to throw up and it might be more successful. WRONG!

I had the dry heaves. Just the smell would get me heaving. I couldn't get the stuff near my nose; every time I smelled it, I had to run to the bathroom. My mother said to plug my nose with one hand while I tried to hold the glass in the other and drink it. It worked except that I couldn't gulp it down like she wanted me to. I had to take a breath between each swallow; which made the whole ordeal last way too long! Finally, I managed to drink the entire contents of the glass and it didn't come back up. Pinching my nose worked.

I was supposed to drink that horrid stuff three times a day; it was torture. After a couple days of endurance, I told mom that I would like to try it straight out of the bottle and then drink some juice to wash it down. She had to call the doctor to see if that was alright. He thought that the taste would be unbearable, but that if I could tolerate it, and thought it was easier, there was no harm. I asked for orange juice to wash it down because it had a stronger flavor than apple juice and I thought it would work better. I was right; I was able to hold my breath and swallow the horrid liquid in one gulp. I then washed the nasty stuff down with some nice, cold orange juice. I was going to be able to survive the next few weeks after all.

I don't actually remember feeling better. What I do remember was not feeling sick. It was summer time and I was busy playing with my friends and neighbors. It was torture to have to go home in the middle of the day to drink my vitamin drink. However, I did it because I was basically an obedient child and didn't want to cause my mother any grief. I know she had her hands full with my brothers.

I remember that my oldest brother was into a lot of trouble all the time. It seemed like he was always being sent to a home for boys called, "Green Hill." It was a place for boys that broke the law and were too young to go to jail. I remember going to visit him there and how he cried and wanted Mom to get him out of there; he broke my heart. There was nothing Mom could do, or maybe she was wise and chose not to do anything because she knew he would get into trouble again. Jerry could not get into trouble when he was in Green Hill.

My brother Warren was acting strange. He didn't like to eat with the rest of the family; he was afraid of our germs. He would eat his meals on the pull-out bread board in the kitchen, while the rest of us sat together at the dining room table. If one of us had to go into the kitchen to get something while he was eating, he would cover his plate with his body and his arms.

He also wanted his clothes washed separately from the rest of us. Luckily, Mom got a new washing machine and no longer had to feed the clothes through the wringer after washing them and then again after rinsing them. The new washing machine had a spin tub! She could put the wet cloths into the spin tub after they washed and the tub would spin them almost dry! (Looking back it still was a lot of work for my mother, but certainly easier than the old wringer.) She got an automatic dryer too! That was sad because we lost a kitty who chose to take a nap in the dryer!

My younger brother had lots of problems. I remember hearing Mom talking on the phone to one of her friends about watching his eye surgery at the children's orthopedic hospital. She said they allowed her to go up and sit in the viewing room for the OR. She said she saw his eyeball laying outside his head, on the side of his face! It sounded terrible, but after the patch came off his eye, it no longer looked out toward the side of his head. He still needed speech therapy, but wasn't going to get that help until he went to school. He had lots of problems, although I really wasn't aware of what they were. He was almost five years old and couldn't do the things I could do when I was five. (At the time, I just thought that girls were smarter than boys.)

My dad was going to Alaska every spring and summer. He would come home in August. He usually didn't get come home until after my little brother and I celebrated our birthdays. Our birthdays were only one day apart, but separated by three years. This summer things were going to be very different!

I was taking my vitamin drink. I hated it, but I drank it. I drank the whole bottle! Then horror of horrors, I had to drink another bottle! After two bottles, the doctor pronounced me strong enough to have a tonsillectomy. The date for my surgery was set, only a few days ahead. The doctor didn't want to take any chances of me catching something or coming down with another bout of pneumonia before he could remove my troublesome tonsils.

Once more he smiled at me and said, "You are going to feel like a brand, new person after your tonsils are out."

I was nervous and couldn't sleep very well for the next few days. Dad came home from Alaska early; he would be home for my tonsillectomy and our birthdays. Was that good news or bad? He acted happy to be home and played horsey with my little sister on his leg and horsey with my little brother on his back. I was too big and mature to play horsey; he just held me close and read me stories.

CHAPTER 52

The Tonsils Come Out

THE NIGHT BEFORE my tonsils were going to be removed, I could not sleep. It was absolutely the worse night I had ever had since I could remember back. Even at my young age, I knew I could remember things from when I was three that my friends and family could not remember. I guess I was like an elephant! (I wondered if an elephant had tonsils.)

I tossed and turned, got up numerous times to check the clock, waited to see if the ghost would make an appearance, and thought of rhyming words. I was extremely nervous, but didn't want to tell anyone because my older brothers would tease me and I didn't want to worry my mom and dad. (It's so hard to be almost eight years old and feel like you need to be big when inside you feel really small. I was very small for my age and looked like I was about six years old. I felt that young or even younger that night.)

Eventually, the light of dawn made its way in through my bedroom window. I got up and looked over at the Tribe's field and toward the water and the mountains. The sun was shining on the Olympics and they were slightly pink in the early morning, even the blue sky above them had a pink tint to it. I loved the colors pink and blue; my room had pink walls and a blue floor. I looked around at my room and I looked again out at the mountains, the sky, and the water. I began to think I might not ever see them again. I looked at the house where the Tribe lived and wondered if I would ever play with those boys again. Tears welled up in my eyes and I silently cried, wishing the day had never come.

I went to my playroom. I had a really nice playroom. My dad had made my dolls a crib, a high chair, and a little closet for my doll clothes. I didn't play with my dolls so much anymore because I played a lot with the Tribe next door. However, this morning I wanted to hold Suzabella and Sweet Sue. I couldn't get enough of their pretty faces, their pretty hair, and their familiar smell. (Their smell was a plastic, artificial smell that caused me asthma if I breathed it too much, but we didn't know that at the time.) I played with my dolls and made sure that they were dressed and sitting properly for everyone to see them. (I wanted them to look really nice in case I didn't come back.)

Pretty soon Mom came up to see if I was awake. She was surprised to find me in the playroom.

"How long have you been up?" She acted happy and smiling, so I knew she was scared too. She didn't wait for my response, she just went on telling me to put on clean underwear and pajamas and to wear my shoes and socks. She was scaring me more; I would have been less frightened if I could put my play clothes on. Sometimes Mom made things worse.

After changing my clothes and washing my face, brushing my teeth, and brushing my hair, I went downstairs. Mom and dad were in the kitchen with David and Susy. My older brothers were still in their bedroom; they were sharing the room for a while. Mom was getting breakfast ready for the family. I wasn't allowed to eat or drink anything, so I sat on a chair and suffered in silence. I wasn't a bit hungry because I was too scared to eat. (Another few years and that would change; I would eat when I was apprehensive about anything.)

My older brothers came down to breakfast when Mom had it cooked and was serving it up to Dad and my little brother and sister. Dad said it was about time they got out of bed. My brother Warren immediately began teasing me about getting my tonsils out. He told me about all the times people died on the operating table because the doctor made a mistake. He told me about people never waking up after they had been put to sleep. He was really frightening me. My stomach was in knots and I wanted to cry, but didn't dare. My brother Jerry told him to shut up and when he didn't, Jerry socked him in the arm!

That started the two of them having a morning wrestle. Mom kept yelling at them to stop and even Dad told them more than once to go outside if they were going to carry on like wild Indians. Pretty soon they were laughing and just having fun. Their wrestling had led them into the dining room and now they came back into the kitchen to get their breakfast. They were in a hurry to eat and be gone to hang out with their various friends for the day. (They had different friends because there were five years difference between them.)

No one took the time to tell me that I would be OK and that I would come home after my tonsils were removed. My mind was filled with fear and with sadness. I looked around at my family (even my annoying little brother) and wondered if I would ever see them again. My little sister was still so small, I never even got to play with her like a friend. She was like a living doll; I could carry her, dress her, rock her and now that she was older I could hold her hand when we went somewhere. Sadly, we never had the opportunity to hang out like girlfriends.

Suddenly Mom said it was time to go. I felt my heart go up into my throat. I could hear my heart beating in my ears. I took a deep breath and said okay like it was just an ordinary day. Mom got on her hat and gloves (she always wore a hat and gloves when she went somewhere) and got her purse. Just Mom and I were going to the Winslow Clinic; Dad was staying home with my little brother and sister. Mom and I walked out the kitchen door, through the utility room, and out the back door. The Pontiac was parked just at the bottom of the stairs. I was wobbling as I climbed down the stairs; I was terrified!

Mom held the door open for me and I climbed into the front seat. She went around the back of the car and opened the front door on her side and climbed in. She was smiling and talking about nothing of any importance to me. I saw her hands shaking as she placed them on the steering wheel and I knew she was scared like me. (Nowadays people talk about their fears, but back then we just pretended we were brave.) We drove to Winslow with Mom talking the whole way, while I sat in silence, not listening to a word she was saying. I was wondering if I would be like the people my brother told me about. I was wondering if my ghost would go back to my house. (I even thought that if my ghost did go back to the house, I would be sure to scare Warren!)

We arrived at the Winslow Clinic all too soon. Mom parked the car in the special parking lot on the side of the building, instead of in front on the street where regular patients' park. Mom told me that because I was having surgery and we would be there for several hours, we were parking in the special parking lot. She said we would only be there for several hours; just that phrase gave me a glimmer of hope! She got out of the car and came around and opened the door for me. I climbed out, my heart beating so hard I thought it would break through my chest. We walked in through the backdoor of the clinic.

The nurse saw us as we came into the hallway. She said good morning and asked how I was feeling. I lied and said fine. She said in a little while I would be waking up and be able to eat all the popsicles I wanted. That sounded pretty good, except I was feeling cold. (The clinic always felt so cold to me.) She escorted us into an examination room where she took my temperature. She smiled and said the doctor would be in momentarily. Usually that would mean we would wait quite a while; this morning he came in within a matter of seconds! He was wearing his white smock with his stethoscope around his neck. He said, "Let's have a listen to your heart."

I didn't know why he always said, "Let's," when he was the only one who listened. He said my heart sounded very strong and he turned to my mother and told her I was scared. He turned back to me, and with his biggest smile, told me that after I woke up from my tonsillectomy that my throat would be very sore. He told me not to try and talk, just to chew as much ice as I could and then eat as many popsicles as I could. He said the more cold things I ate, the better my throat would feel. He said that after my throat healed I would feel like a brand new person and that I wouldn't get sick anymore. Then he said, "Let's get this done!"

The nurse came into the examination room pushing another table or bed; I really couldn't tell what it was, just that it was cold metal with a paper sheet stretched over it. She said to climb over and lay down on my back. I did, acting much braver than I felt. Then she wheeled me into another room. I had been to the clinic many times over the years, but I didn't recognize that room at all. There was a very bright light hanging overhead.

The doctor and the nurse had changed their smocks and had on greenish gray smocks. They had white masks over their faces and only their eyes showed above them. The nurse put something that looked like Mom's little kitchen strainer over my nose and mouth and told me to close my eyes and to count backwards from 10. I was too curious and scared, and refused to close my eyes! I watched as the nurse took a little bottle and poured the contents over the strainer that was on my face. She told me to count. I smelled this horrid smell and saw the nurse's head spinning around like a record on a record player!

I counted, "ten, nine, eight, sev. . . ."

The next thing I was aware of was a voice in the far distance saying, "Wake up Vicki, wake up Vicki."

I was still alive! My throat hurt like crazy, but I was alive and the nurse was offering me chopped ice to suck on. That meant soon I would have as many popsicles as I could eat! If what the doctor said was true, I wasn't going to get sick anymore. I wondered what my life would be like from then on; I was already filled with anticipation and looking forward to new adventures.

Epilogue

Join Vicki as she emerges into a new found life of health and wellbeing. No longer plagued by allergies, asthma, and the biannual bouts of pneumonia, she faces life with enthusiasm and fascination. More friends, frolics, and adventures await as she moves forward with, "Full Steam Ahead."

About the Author

Victoria Farnsworth was born in California, but grew up on a beautiful island in the Pacific Northwest. She spent three years in California as a teenager, but returned to the Pacific Northwest to graduate from high school. It was during her senior year that she met her husband, and after his return from Viet Nam, they married. They have spent over 44 years together and have three married daughters and eight beautiful (and highly intelligent) grandchildren. Due to health reasons, Victoria has moved to Payson and is enjoying her retirement surrounded by the natural beauty of the mountains in central Arizona.

She had her first work published in the Reader's Digest in August of 1983. She spent the next several years writing poems for family, friends, and church, but never endeavoring to publish her work. She kept busy working as a secretary for the Department of the Navy for several years. She then spent the next 15 years teaching swimming and related aquatic classes for various school and park districts in the states of Washington, Oregon, and California.

During her years working outside the home, she was also busy raising a family of three girls. As is every mother, she was busy driving girls to lessons, sports, and church activities. She had to deal with teenage boys, lovesick girls, and being married to a millworker turned truck driver.

When all the girls left home for school or marriage, rather than feel like an empty nester, she spent time in serious prayer and contemplation. She then embarked on a new career path, and became Clara the Clown. Seven years were spent clowning around up and down the West Coast. As always, she was busy with church service, and managed to be a Relief Society President during this time. Her new career ended when a car accident forced her to retire. After becoming a Master Gardener, she started a new business doing landscape design. Unfortunately, another car accident forced her to once again give up something she loved.

Writing continued to be a hobby. During her 10 year membership in the Glove & Trowel Garden Club, she spent 4 years as secretary and writing the quarterly update of the club's activities. In June of 2011 Victoria had an article published in the Northwest Landscape Professional magazine about butterfly gardening. So many people read the article and commented that she should write professionally; a seed was planted! She kept an online journal of her life in Mexico, and continues with a website devoted to her new life and home in Payson, Arizona.

As time has passed, Victoria has received more opportunities to relate stories from her life. Each time, people comment that she should write a book. Now, in her retirement, the time has come to share her life experiences. One book could not begin to hold 60 plus years of unforgettable events; hence this work will take many volumes to tell the story of an ordinary woman living an extraordinary life.

20416322R00087

Made in the USA
San Bernardino, CA
10 April 2015